About the Book

It is possible that man's very survival may soon depend upon the resources of the sea. Covering nearly three-fourths of the earth's surface and still largely unexplored, the oceans comprise a vast and mysterious domain that shelter a treasure trove of food, fuel, and other resources needed by the people of the world.

The ocean depths give up their secrets grudgingly, but hidden among them may be the answers to many questions about earth's origin and the restless nature of its crust. Drilling into the deep-sea floor from rigs aboard large research vessels is now in operation, and specially designed submersibles are probing earth's darkest quarters. Perhaps even a new lifestyle is being developed as aquanauts find the shallow marine floors more and more hospitable for temporary dwelling.

The search, however, has just begun. This book explores the promising frontier that the oceans present, as well as the variety of careers opening up for young men and women. It guides the reader through the depths and shallows of the oceans to discover the awesome variety of seascapes, the teeming life beneath the surface, and the rich promise of these hidden worlds.

THE STORY OF
OCEANOGRAPHY

BY ROBERT E. BOYER

HARVEY HOUSE • NEW YORK • NEW YORK

To my wife, Betty

Library of Congress Catalog Card Number 74-25425
Manufactured in the United States of America
ISBN 0-8178-5141-0, Trade edition; ISBN 0-8178-5142-9, Library edition

Harvey House, New York, New York
A Division of E. M. Hale & Company
Eau Claire, Wisconsin

Contents

Preface

This book is about our last frontier on earth — the oceans. They are strange and forbidding worlds, but worlds that may supply mankind with vital resources for continued life on earth. Their hidden wealth includes a variety of minerals, and more important, a supply of food and fresh water. Therein lies the challenge, for man must develop the technology to harvest the riches of the sea.

Living throughout the oceans is a vast array of organisms, ranging from billions of single-celled, microscopic plants to the largest mammals on earth. They abound along the shoreline and on the shelves of the continents. Here, amidst the filtering sunlight of the shallow waters, lies the jungle of the seas. However, life extends to the deepest, darkest corners of the ocean bottom where miniature monsters dwell.

Buried beneath this watery blanket is a land that contains some of the flattest plains, deepest canyons and highest mountains in the world. Oceanographers believe that here are the answers to problems which have plagued earth scientists for centuries. An understanding of why earthquakes occur, the origin of mountains, and even how the continents form and gradually change may be revealed through study of the ocean basins.

Hopefully, readers of this book will find the ocean world an exciting one, and will have a new appreciation for its value. Perhaps some readers will be encouraged to accept the challenge of an exciting career in oceanography as man seeks to develop the oceans during the last quarter of the twentieth century.

The author is indebted to many people who helped make this book a reality. Illustrations were obtained from a number of sources; these are acknowledged on each photograph. I would especially like to thank Robert E. Johnson, Jr. of the U.S. Naval Oceanographic Office; Dr. Lynton S. Land of The University of Texas at Austin; Keith L. Simmons of the Oceanographic Sorting Center, Smithsonian Institution; and William O. West of the National Oceanic and Atmospheric Administration; who greatly aided my search for illustrations. Donald P. Erickson and Wayne E. Jones prepared the line drawings.

Thanks are also due to Dr. Judith C. Lang, Smithsonian Tropical Research Institute, and Wayne R. Schade, Education Service Center, Austin, Texas, who read the manuscript and offered helpful suggestions, and Mrs. Jeanne Gardner of Harvey House, Inc., for her patience, understanding, and editorial assistance in the preparation of the manuscript. I am especially indebted to Prof. William H. Matthews III of Lamar University who suggested that I write this book. Finally, I thank my wife, Betty; without her encouragement and understanding this book could not have been written.

R. E. B.

1

Monsters of the Deep

Picture, if you can, a creature having an eighteen-foot body with a parrot-like beak surrounded by eight arms, each about six feet long. Two rope-like tentacles as thick as a man's body reach out some forty feet from its head. It moves cautiously along, only to be snapped up by a more ferocious beast that is ten times its size. The predator has eight-inch daggerlike teeth and powerful jaws set in a head over twenty feet long.

Monsters from a prehistoric past? Not quite. They survive today where no man lives and few dare to visit. In contrast to the hot steamy jungles of Africa and South America, where you might expect to find strange beasts, they dwell in the cold depths of the oceans, for they are the giant squid and his chief enemy, the sperm whale. These are but two of the many curious creatures found in the seas where life on our planet first began.

The variety of ocean life is incredible. Microscopic animals and plants, many so tiny that it would require 1000 side by side to be one inch long, drift with the ocean currents and provide food for fish and sea creatures. Some types of organisms attach themselves to the floor of the sea or crawl along it. Others are predominantly swimmers and

Courtesy Mrs. Poul H. Winthers, The Galathea Deep Sea Expedition, 1950-52

A living "mouse-trap," this strange fish of the deep has a forked light organ hanging from the roof of its mouth. The light attracts its unsuspecting victims. This deep-sea angler, the only specimen of its kind ever captured, was dredged from 12,960 feet in the ocean.

live in the shallow water near the shores, at all depths in the ocean waters, and along the ocean bottoms. About 20,000 different types of fish — ranging from small minnows to some larger than a cow — are found in the oceans. Despite their abundance, however, fish are vastly outnumbered by the many types of sea animals without backbones. The oceans abound with life and offer mankind a major source of food.

New Clues to Old Mysteries

Ancient legends tell of a mysterious land where people lived a life of comfort over 3000 years ago. They had stone houses with hot and cold running water and air conditioning systems that channeled cool breezes into their rooms through open passageways. These people built ocean-going ships, forged metal tools, designed ornate pottery and developed an irrigation system to water their crops. They even had ample time for boxing, wrestling and other sporting events. Unfortunately for later civilizations, these people and their land — known as Atlantis — disappeared from the face of the earth.

About 400 B.C., the curious and wise Greek philosopher, Plato, studied the legends about these people. He decided that the lost Atlantis was a continent in the Atlantic Ocean beyond the Old World. Later philosophers said that horses and elephants and strange beasts of the past used Atlantis to reach North America from Europe, and that primitive man traveled this path, too.

For centuries scientists and historians have searched unsuccessfully for traces of this missing land. Today, many of them doubt that it ever existed. Probably, they say, Atlantis was an island near Greece that blew apart in a mighty volcanic explosion sometime about 1500 B.C. and collapsed into the sea. The truth of the story may lie buried under a hundred feet of volcanic rocks on a part of this island that still remains. Here scientists have uncovered tools, pottery shards, and fire-blackened walls of stone houses similar to those described in the legends about the early civilization of Atlantis. Final proof, however, may exist only in sunken lands on a lower level of the ocean floor.

Atlantis is but one of the many mysteries awaiting underwater exploration. Indeed, the oceans represent our last earthly frontier for, although man has walked in space and visited the moon, he has never set foot on the deep ocean floor.

The search for Atlantis has led oceanographers to discover a chain of mountains buried by the Atlantic Ocean. These prominent underwater peaks and ridges extend along nearly the entire length of the ocean, splitting it in two. Similar ridges have also been found in the Indian and Pacific oceans. Perhaps these hidden mountain chains mark

Man probes the ocean depths in search of information. Here oceanographers lower a deep-sea camera over the side of a Navy research vessel.

world-wide fractures in the earth's crust and the beginnings of future ocean floors. They may even provide important clues about changing shapes and shifting positions of continents through geologic time.

The Last Frontier

Scientists are just beginning to understand the part of the earth's crust hidden by the oceans. They realize, too, that man has not fully developed the sea's potential for food and mineral resources. The seas are truly becoming more important as the world population continues to grow.

Concentration of people in cities accentuates the need for food and water. Fresh water is already in short supply in some areas. Newspaper accounts about conservation efforts and pollution of our land stress the necessity for greater utilization of the oceans as a source of food and water. Through careful use, the oceans may furnish some of our critical needs. It is possible to foresee desalination (salt removal) plants dotting major coastlines and piping usable water to inland cities.

Oceanographers recognize the delicate balance of nature. They know that not all the answers to our ecologic problems lie in conquering the mystery and awesome power of the oceans. They realize, however, that the oceans contain vast resources that are as yet untapped. They know, too, that valuable elements are held in solution in sea water which someday may be withdrawn and used. These scientists also recognize the importance of maintaining clean oceans and preventing their pollution because man will become more dependent upon our great seas as each year passes.

Planet earth, a world predominated by water, viewed from an altitude of 22,300 miles by NASA's Applications Technology Satellite. Left view over Pacific Ocean; right view shows North and South Atlantic.

Courtesy National Aeronautics and Space Administration

2

The Oceans Are Born

Earth was a hot and hostile world, void of atmosphere and oceans some four and one-half billion years ago. For a long time, perhaps a billion years, our planet slowly cooled through a molten state and its surface gradually became solid rock. One widely supported view is that during this interval, water vapor and other gases were released from the earth's interior and accumulated as a cloud-like envelope surrounding the cooling mass to form a primitive atmosphere. The rate at which this leakage of gases, called *degassing,* took place is a matter of controversy among scientists. Some favor a rapid spewing out of gases during a time of fast temperature change. More than likely, however, these vapors escaped slowly through intermittent volcanic activity, continuing for many millions of years as the earth's outer zones gradually cooled.

Dense clouds laden with moisture formed in the earth's young atmosphere as more and more steam was released at the surface. Rain fell from the clouds, and water slowly accumulated as the surface rocks cooled. The water flowed downslope until it reached the low places to create the first seas on earth. The rains continued for many thousands, probably millions, of years, and the seas gradually grew larger. In fact it may have taken well over a billion years for the oceans to approach their present size — or they may have been growing steadily throughout geologic time and are growing even now.

Thus from a planet with bare rock surface, earth gradually changed to the water planet we live on today, with a blanket of water covering nearly 71 percent of its surface. Our present oceans are a "salty" mixture containing a great variety of minerals and salts locked in solution. However, when our planet was only a billion years old, it was made up of less salty water.

Pioneers of the Sea

Man's first encounter with the seas dates back some million years when primitive man first wandered along the beaches hunting clams and spearing fish. The sea remained a mystic thing to be feared and worshipped, for it surely contained gigantic and deadly monsters. After all, were not the daily fluctuations of the sea — the tides — caused by the breathing of these giant sea serpents!

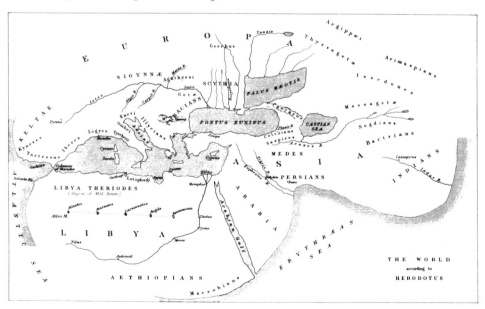

The world through the eyes of Herodotus (about 450 B.C.) showed Europe and Asia as a continuous land mass surrounded by seas.

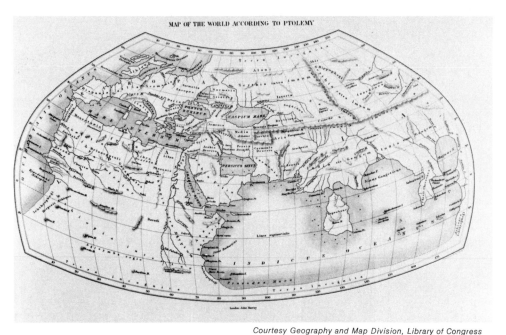

Ptolemy (about 150 A.D.) viewed the world with Asia exaggerated and the Atlantic Ocean too narrow.

Earliest records show that man pictured earth as a flat surface with swirling waters circling the land. In the fifth century B. C., however, the Greek historian, Herodotus, visualized the earth as a sphere divided into temperature zones and largely covered by vast oceans. About 250 B. C., Eratosthenes accepted the concept of earth as a sphere and calculated its circumference to be about 28,500 miles, a remarkably good estimate for that time.

In the second century A. D., the Egyptian, Ptolemy, envisioned the Atlantic Ocean to be largely surrounded by land. But before Ptolemy's theory could be tested, the earth again became flat in the minds of men who were strongly influenced by religious beliefs then prevalent. Seafarers were frightened by prophesies that they would fall off the earth or meet some terrible fate if they strayed from familiar coastal waters. Indeed, science was all but forgotten. Very little new was learned about the oceans for nearly a thousand years. This period was appropriately called the *Dark Ages,* during which scientific study was discouraged or even punished.

16

Only the Chinese traveled extensively on the seas at this time. They traded with East Africa as early as 860 A.D., and by the 15th century had trade relations with many countries in the western Pacific Ocean.

Fortunately, fears and superstitions came to a dramatic end in Europe in the 1400's when Portuguese ships crept down the African coast in search of a sea route to India. One ship ventured farther than the rest and was swept around the southern tip of Africa when it was caught in hurricane winds reported to have lasted for thirteen days. Its sailors returned to Portugal to proclaim that they had encountered no boiling seas, swirling bottomless pits, or edges of the world.

And so the spell was broken. Courageous navigators set sail for far-off lands. Columbus, Magellan, Ponce de Leon, and others explored the seas during the sixteenth and seventeenth centuries. Maps of the world changed quickly as ships crossed and recrossed the seas. One especially important finding revealed that the oceans are interconnected, while land masses are not. Features about the surface waters were recorded on many of these trips, resulting in much better understanding of tides, the positions of major currents, and the pattern of water temperatures. But the focus was on traveling the seas, not studying them.

The Birth of Oceanography

The direction of interest changed when the British seaman and scientist, Captain James Cook, pioneered sea investigations with three voyages starting in 1768 on the Pacific Ocean. Captain Cook's accurate records of winds and currents, his temperature tests, and depth measurements to 1200 feet marked a beginning of the scientific study known as oceanography.

Two naturalists of the eighteenth and nineteenth centuries stand out as "founding fathers" of modern oceanography. Britisher Edward Forbes became fascinated with marine life and suggested that different

A U.S. expedition (1838-42) on the 88-foot brig *Porpoise* covered 90,000 miles, surveyed 280 islands and discovered that Antarctica was a continent.

animals live at various depths within the oceans. Matthew Maury served in the U.S. Navy and collected and plotted observations on winds and currents reported from Navy ships. He produced a series of charts on the general directions and strengths of current and wind patterns. Maury also measured the shape of the North Atlantic sea floor. He used an improved sounding device with a detachable weight that signaled the settling of a line lowered to the ocean bottom. Based on his maps, the first international cables were laid down linking America and Europe.

One hundred years ago the H.M.S. *Challenger* of the British Admiralty logged nearly 69,000 miles with detailed recordings at over 350 locations during a three-and-a-half year voyage. Myriads of new and fascinating life forms were dredged from water as deep as 25,000 feet. Seventy-seven water samples were taken, and temperature readings at depths below 12,000 feet revealed the icy cold waters there. The importance of the *Challenger* expedition prompted the statement: "Never did an expedition cost so little and produce such momentous results for human knowledge."

Fascinated by the many puzzling problems about the seas, Alexander Agassiz traveled over 100,000 miles on oceanographic voyages during the years 1877-1907. Using the famous U.S. *Albatross,* the first ship built especially for oceanographic exploration, Agassiz studied the physical and biological conditions of the oceans. His interest in marine life led to a scientific approach to fishing and eventually resulted in commercial fisheries. Thus with its roots firmly anchored in science, the field of oceanography moved into the twentieth century.

The H.M.S. *Challenger* pioneered ocean studies with an historic voyage.

Report of Voyage of H.M.S. Challenger

Report of Voyage of H.M.S. Challenger

Dredging and sounding equipment on board the H.M.S. *Challenger.*

3

Our Salty Seas

Water is the most amazing liquid on earth. Imagine a world where water becomes denser as it freezes. Ice cubes would automatically sink in a glass of water. There would be no ice skating because lakes and ponds would freeze from the bottom up.

All life in the waters would undoubtedly be killed if the bottoms of ponds, lakes, and the oceans filled with ice first. Circulation in the oceans would quickly be interrupted, or prevented, and life as we know it would never have developed on earth. Fortunately for us, water is one of a very few liquids that *expands* when it freezes.

Water has other remarkable and fascinating properties. It is one of only three substances that occurs naturally as a liquid (oil and un-combined mercury are the others). Water also has the important property of dissolving more substances and in greater amounts than most other liquids. It is no wonder that seawater has commonly been called a weak solution of "almost everything." It contains a complex mixture of dissolved solids and gases which scientists believe includes every element known.

Surprisingly, despite its strong salty taste, seawater is 96.5 percent pure H_2O. But still there are about 50,000,000,000,000,000 (50 quadrillion) tons of dissolved salts making up the remaining 3.5 percent of the oceans. That amounts to about 166 million tons of salts dissolved in each cubic mile of seawater. If all the substances in solution were removed from the oceans, they would bury earth's entire land surface with a blanket 500 feet thick, which is about as high as a 40-story building. But where did all the salts come from?

MAIN DISSOLVED SUBSTANCES IN SEAWATER[*]

Water	965,000 ppm
Chlorine	19,000 ppm
Sodium	10,500 ppm
Magnesium	1,300 ppm
Sulfate	885 ppm
Calcium	400 ppm
Potassium	380 ppm
Bromine	65 ppm
Carbon	30 ppm
Strontium	10 ppm
Boron	4.5 ppm
Silica	3 ppm
Fluorine	1 ppm
All others less than	1 ppm

Amount of each substance given in parts per million (ppm) which means the number of parts of that substance in a million parts of seawater.

Since the seas first formed, they have been a resting place for the water carried by rivers flowing over the land. Rivers contain a vast quantity of loose, fine rock debris, organic matter, and substances in solution. The Mississippi River alone pours solid and dissolved material into the Gulf of Mexico at the rate of 2,000,000 tons per day. The material comes from the land surface where rocks are being broken into finer and finer particles by the never-ending process called *weathering*. Rain washes over the land, carrying the fine particles and dissolved substances to the rivers, which transport them to the sea.

Volcanoes, too, contribute gaseous and solid matter to the oceans. Add to this fine meteorite debris and other material blown in from the land. Still other contributing sources come from the activity of life within the sea and from dissolved skeletons of calcareous animals which fall into deep water. Through millions and millions of years, material has been added to the seas and they have gradually changed to the salty solution existing today.

Courtesy Oceanographer of the Navy

An oceanographer aboard ship taps water from ocean samples for study in the laboratory.

Despite the variety of sources, however, most substances in seawater occur in extremely minor amounts. In addition to oxygen and hydrogen, by far the most abundant elements are sodium and chlorine. If all the water in a single cubic mile of seawater is evaporated, over 49 million tons of sodium and 89 million tons of chlorine would remain. This explains why the term *salinity* (meaning the total of all dissolved salts in solution) is frequently misunderstood to mean simply the amount of our common table salt, sodium chloride, in seawater when it really includes probably every known element on earth.

A Thirsty World

Earth contains about 320 million cubic miles of seawater — a whopping 97 percent of all the water in the world — and it is all salty! Most of the remaining water lies frozen, mainly on Antarctica and Greenland. Man presently survives on fresh water, which is less than one percent of the world's total water supply.

Demands for this fresh water are great. Agriculture, industry, city needs, and water for everyday living all add up to a tremendous thirst. The United States alone requires about 390 billion gallons of water each day. About 400,000 gallons are needed to grow a ton of corn, and it takes 800 gallons just to produce one loaf of bread. Incredible as it may seem, each person in the United States uses an average of over 60 gallons of water daily for drinking, washing, and other household purposes. It is no wonder that man looks yearningly to the seas as a source of fresh water.

The serious water shortage on earth is becoming greater every day, especially in the world's big cities. One reason is the expanding demand for water. In the United States, for instance, the use of water is increasing at the fantastic rate of 25,000 gallons per *minute!* Parts of the world are destined to run out of fresh water before the end of the twentieth century. *Desalination,* the process of changing seawater to fresh water, may solve this problem.

Desalting of seawater has already been done. The trick is to do it cheaply so that costs of the treated water are not too high. Residents of St. Thomas on the Virgin Islands and Key West, Florida, are already drinking water from the sea. In fact, over 500 desalination plants are now operating throughout the world.

This desalination plant at Freeport, Texas, produces 900,000 gallons of fresh water per day.

Several techniques may be used for the desalting process. One popular way, called *distillation,* is to heat seawater until it evaporates and then collect the steam. When condensed to liquid, the water is free of salts. Another method which seems promising involves the passing of seawater through a very thin mesh (membrane). Water molecules are able to pass through but the dissolved salts are not, and in this way the water is purified. Still a third process, successful in converting salty water

24

at Buckeye, Arizona, uses an electric current to attract the dissolved salts from the water.

Fresh water is undoubtedly one of the most important resources of the oceans. Perhaps by the year 2000, every major coastal city will depend heavily upon seawater for its fresh water supply.

An unwelcome intruder on the high seas may help to solve the water shortage. One night in April 1912, the British steamer *Titanic* sank on its first voyage across the Atlantic Ocean. The *Titanic* had struck an iceberg! These floating piers of ice have always been a menace to seafarers. An International Ice Patrol plots their paths as they drift south from Greenland into the Gulf Stream — an estimated 7,500 bergs each year.

Across the continent, some thirsty southern Californians look yearningly to Antarctica for its supply of icebergs. Here lies a wealth of fresh water, researchers claim. Lassoed with cables and wrapped in plastic to protect them from sea water erosion, a train of icebergs can be readily towed north to California's coastal cities. The trip would take about ten months using nuclear-powered tugboats to tow the bergs to mooring areas. Perhaps a sea menace will eventually prove useful to mankind.

Icebergs like this one are a danger to shipping as they float south from Greenland into the Gulf Stream of the North Atlantic Ocean.

Courtesy Oceanographer of the Navy

A seaman lowers bathythermograph into the water to take temperature readings.

The Weight of Water

The British naturalist, Edward Forbes, insisted that no life existed below 1800 feet, when he outlined the eight life zones in the Mediterranean Sea in the mid-nineteenth century. After all, how could any creature live in such a bleak environment that was eternally dark with temperatures hovering near freezing? Certainly no forms of life could withstand the terrible forces of water pressure — enough to crush into powder the thermometers lowered to such depths.

Not so, exclaimed scientists aboard the *Challenger* expedition, for their dredging proved that abundant fish and other creatures inhabited the briny deep. But the riddle remained. How could living things withstand the pressures at the oceans' great depths?

Pressure increases at the rate of 14.7 pounds to the square inch with every 33 feet in depth. That means a creature crawling along the ocean floor, 12,000 feet below the surface, withstands the incredible weight of nearly three tons over each square inch of its body.

Deep-sea animals contain body fluids which have the same tremendous pressure as the surrounding water. Because the liquids within the body press outward with the same force, everything balances. Man does not have this built-in protection because living in deep water is not his natural habitat. Diving is therefore limited to shallow depths and return to the surface must be done slowly. If the pressure changes too fast, air in the lungs may expand too fast and cause lung explosion, or the diver may get the *bends,* caused by nitrogen in his bloodstream bubbling up. In contrast, some sea animals are protected so that they can move freely between areas of different pressure. Whales dive swiftly to depths of 1200 feet and more without injury.

Marine life photographed at a depth of more than three miles in the Atlantic Ocean. Left: the deepest octopus ever pictured. Right: the first photograph of a rare multi-cellular animal similar to sea anemone and coral.

Courtesy U.S. Naval Oceanographic Office

A Nansen bottle is connected to a line to obtain sample of sea water.

Sampling the Ocean Deep

Surface temperature of the oceans may be a chilling 30°F in the polar regions and a warm 85°F or higher in the tropics. Water temperature also changes at different levels within the oceans. Temperature drops steadily from the surface to a depth of some 2,500 feet where it reaches several degrees above the freezing point of seawater. From there the temperature drops slowly to the ocean deep, reaching as low as 28°F, just barely above the freezing point of seawater.

Aboard the *Challenger,* taking temperature readings and water samples were difficult tasks. Men labored many hours just to haul up the heavy cable for one sample. Today these readings and samples are obtained quickly and accurately. One popular way is to use a hollow cylinder, called a *Nansen Bottle,* with valves at each end. The cylinder is attached to a cable lowered to the right depth. When a weight, known as a *messenger,* moves down the line, it releases a clamp. The bottle then tips over and shuts off the valves, trapping the water in the cylinder.

Thermometers protected from the oceanic pressures may also be attached to the Nansen bottles. When the bottles flip over, exact temperatures can be recorded at the time the water is sampled. Some thermometers are designed to be exposed to abnormally high pressures. The temperature readings they record can also be used to determine the high pressures at these depths.

Modern technology permits a moving ship to record a series of continuous temperature measurements from different ocean depths. In this way, models of temperature patterns at all levels within the oceans are made. These are checked from time to time to detect changes related to the seasons or to shifts in ocean currents.

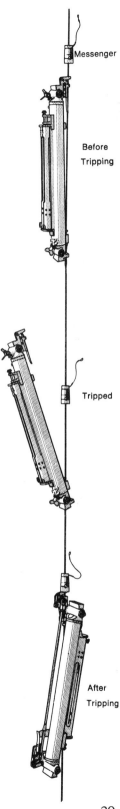

Messenger

Before
Tripping

Tripped

After
Tripping

29

4

The Oceans in Motion

Spanish explorers and merchantmen visiting the New World quickly realized that their fastest return trip was not straight across the Atlantic. Many days traveling time was saved by taking a longer route north from Cuba along the U.S. coastline to Cape Hatteras and then northeastward to Europe.

*   *   *

London, England, is "famous" for pea-soup fog. Similar blankets of dense fog are common marine hazards off the Grand Banks of New-foundland and in the Norwegian Sea.

*   *   *

For years fishermen have steered clear of a wide belt running north-eastward across the Atlantic Ocean. Fish, too, avoid this strip of strikingly blue waters.

*   *   *

England, Norway and other northwestern European countries enjoy a marked degree of warming along their shores. Average winter temperatures are as much as fifteen to twenty degrees Fahrenheit higher than other lands that far north.

*   *   *

These seemingly unrelated conditions are caused by the world's mightiest "river," the Gulf Stream. Yet it is only a part of a giant whirlpool movement in the North Atlantic Ocean. Westward-moving trade winds across the Atlantic pump water between the islands of the West Indies into the Gulf of Mexico. There it piles up until, as a warm water stream, it pours into the Atlantic Ocean between Cuba and Florida.

From its Gulf of Mexico fountain, this river in the ocean flows northward along the United States coastline. Moving more rapidly than the Amazon River, the Gulf Stream carries along 4,000,000,000 tons of water a minute, a thousand times the volume of the Mississippi River. Ships catching this warm, indigo-blue waterway ride its current with increased speed.

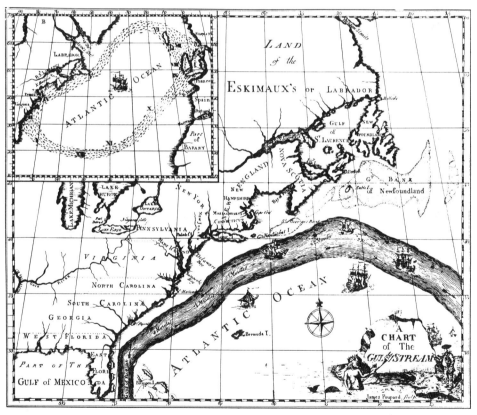

Benjamin Franklin's chart of the Gulf Stream, prepared in 1769, aided ships sailing east across the Atlantic Ocean.

31

Where the warm Gulf Stream veers eastward near Newfoundland, it collides with the icy cold Labrador Currents. Massive clouds of fog result. By the same token, the warm water causes fog when its moisture-laden air drifts over England and the northern European countries. The Gulf Stream also serves to warm the shorelines of these European countries that it touches — resulting in milder temperatures there.

The stream is about fifty miles wide and 1,800 feet deep as it flows northward past Miami, Florida. An abrupt "wall" marks its boundary with the colder waters along the North American coast. This warm water contains less oxygen and food sources than does the adjacent colder water. The Gulf Stream is therefore generally avoided by the schools of fish sought by fishermen patrolling the Atlantic.

Water Currents and Wind Patterns

Restlessness extends throughout the oceans, for all the waters are continually going somewhere. Water that clings to your back when you are surfing in California or New Jersey may well have circled Antarctica and then traveled 10,000 miles before reaching you. This circulation of the oceans is now taken for granted, yet few people would stake their lives to prove this fact in the fashion done by Fridtjof Nansen.

This Norwegian explorer set out in 1893 to follow a current from Siberia across the frozen Arctic to the Atlantic. His scheme was daring — to lock into the polar ice pack and allow the currents to carry ice and ship to the Greenland shores. Moving at a snail's pace of about one mile per day, his brave crew struggled against cold and ice for three years until their ship, the *Fram,* finally broke loose into the Greenland Sea and demonstrated that Arctic currents do indeed move the ice across the top of the world.

A network of streams and currents dissects all portions of the seas. This surface water circulation is set in motion by our spinning globe and modified by contrasts in the warming of the seas between

Courtesy Norwegian Embassy Information Service

The 128-foot *Fram* shown during the three-year cruise of Fridtjof Nansen across the Arctic.

equator and poles. The flow of warm equatorial water toward the poles in exchange for cold polar water is an important feature of the oceans' movement. Added to this is the force of prevailing wind belts that are produced as the earth rotates under its gaseous envelope. In fact, these steady winds tend to drive the waters onward in their giant eddies.

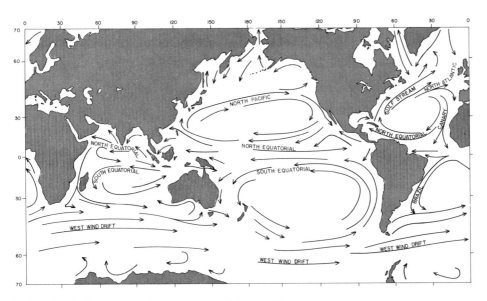

Major circulation patterns in the oceans of the world.

The North Atlantic characterizes this pattern with the Gulf Stream on its western side. The counterpart, the cool Canaries current, flows southward on the east side of the Atlantic. This clockwise-moving whirl dominates the North Atlantic Ocean. The South Atlantic presents a mirror image of this pattern. Similar giant eddies form stirring pots of the Pacific and Indian oceans.

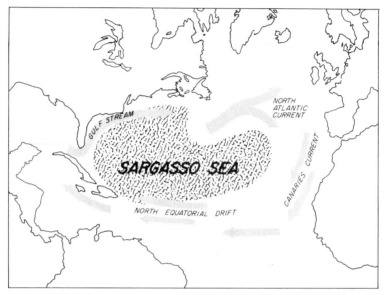

The Sargasso Sea lies at the center of the huge North Atlantic current whirl.

The Sargasso Sea rests inside the North Atlantic whirl. Since the time of Columbus, seafarers have noted abundant patches of floating sea-weed in this slow-moving water. Legends cautioned that captains should steer clear of these weeds lest their ships become entangled forever. In fact, the Sargasso represents a great expanse of barren waters with little marine life. It is a biological desert despite the thin clusters of plant life at its surface.

Creep in the Deep

Tracking deep-ocean currents may prove important in controlling pollution of the oceans. Oceanographers are now studying sea-bottom

34

circulation by adding small amounts of radioactive *tracer* elements to the currents as they sink from the surface. Instruments similar to sensitive stethoscopes pick up the "beat" of these tracers and follow their paths through the seas. In this way man may eventually control the spread of any contaminants that reach the oceans.

Strange creatures inhabit the very bottom of the seas. Because all animal life needs oxygen, circulation of surface water that mixes with the atmosphere and becomes oxygen-rich must extend to all depths. The leisurely flow of these deep-ocean currents, however, makes their location and measurement an extremely difficult task.

Ripple marks, formed by currents on the Atlantic Ocean floor (depth 9,738 feet), photographed during a cruise of USNS *Eltanin*. The compass shows current flow is S. 40° W.

A frogman from the nuclear submarine *Seadragon* taking a picture in the first series ever shot of Arctic ice under the North polar region.

The greatest bottom-water flow begins in the Weddell Sea off Antarctica, where water sinks from the surface and creeps northward toward the equator. In the same manner, cold water near the Arctic moves sluggishly southward as it falls to the ocean depths. These currents are pushed along, like banks of snow in front of a plow, by the continued accumulation of more cold, very dense water behind them. As a result of these movements, fresh oxygen is supplied even to the deepest parts of the oceans, although it may take 1000 years for these same waters to warm up and rise to the surface in other parts of the world.

The Flow of Nutrients

Large schools of commercial fish concentrate where the ocean waters are richest in plant-supporting minerals, called *nutrients*. Plants require these nutrients to produce organic matter. One major source of minerals is from the land surface where rivers pick up this material and dump it into the ocean.

Currents that move the mineral-rich waters also determine locations for successful fishing. Peru, for example, benefits from the Humboldt Current flowing northward along its shores. These cold waters, rich in oxygen and nutrients, attract schools of fish that feed upon the abundant plant life growing there. Because of this current, Peru is among the world leaders in the fishing industry.

The huge catches of the little anchovy fish along the Peruvian coast are rapidly depleting the food sources for the flocks of birds living there. These birds, boobies, cormorants, and pelicans, eat the anchovies and their droppings collect in thick layers on the coastal islands. Since the mid-1800's this *guano* (bird manure) has been collected and sold by Peruvians to earn their livelihood. As fishing industry thrives, the

Huge flocks of birds live along the coast of Peru and feed on the many schools of little fish whose food comes from the nutrient-rich Humboldt Current.

Courtesy Mario Samamé Boggio, Lima, Peru

guano sellers find fewer and fewer birds — and less of the valuable manure. Some of the bird droppings fall into the ocean, adding nutrients for plant growth. The decline of birds may, therefore, hurt the fishing industry too.

Record anchovy catches in 1970 and 1971 have added to another problem. An unpredictable flow of warm Pacific Ocean waters moved south in late 1971, reducing the upwelling of nutrient-rich waters of the Humboldt Current. The number of anchovies was greatly reduced and most fishing was banned for one year. However, the population of these little fish has failed to grow since return of the colder waters. Perhaps the earlier overfishing, coupled with the warm currents, have ended the Peruvian fishing and guano industries for some years to come.

Organic debris collects and decomposes on the ocean floors where bottom-hugging currents pick up these nutrients. As the currents move into tropical regions, they gradually warm up, become lighter, and rise to the surface. The upwellings are laden with food sources important to tiny marine animals and plants on which fish thrive. Schools of fish gather at upwellings along the coasts of northern Florida and California for just this reason.

The Sargasso Sea, in contrast, is poor fishing ground. Surface currents whirl around it and no major upwellings occur within it. This lack of fresh nutrient supply explains the sparsity of biological activity there.

5

The Oceans Alive

Marine life enjoys a three-dimensional world, living all through its environment. It extends from the surface layers, bathed in sunlight and continually refreshed by an oxygen rinse, to the cold, dark isolation of the ocean bottom. Plants and animals exist at all depths of the sea. In contrast, life on land is chained to the floor of an ocean of gases. Few organisms range beyond a foot or two into the soil and rock of the earth's crust. Even the flying creatures are bound by a low ceiling and they must land from time to time.

By far the greatest number of marine organisms are tiny; some, about 1/25,000th of an inch long, can only be seen with a powerful microscope. Others are the largest living creatures on earth, like the blue whale which may grow to a length of 100 feet and weigh 150 tons. Animals can be found that look like plants — complete with organs that resemble roots, stems, and a flowery bloom.

The sea also hosts a number of "living fossils." One that particularly excited scientists was the *coelocanth,* which was first discovered accidentally by a fisherman off the east coast of South Africa in 1938. Distinctive for its paddle-shaped fins, the coelocanth is a close relative

An underwater "garden" of shallow marine animals flourishes in the Caribbean Sea.

of the first amphibians on earth and was thought to be extinct for some 70 million years.

Some animals of the sea are almost totally transparent, while others have internal organs that glow in dark water. The color patterns can be striking, and some sea creatures are able to change to any of eight different colors to match their surroundings.

Within the world of the oceans, this incredible variety of life fiercely competes for survival. There seem to be as many patterns of living in the seas as forms inhabiting it. Some sea animals cruise along at the whims of the currents during youth, then attach to one spot for the rest of their lives. Others have the power to choose their own paths, swimming against currents and moving about at will. Still others are drifters throughout life, always at the mercy of water movement. And yet other organisms live on the sea floors where they may confine themselves to small crevices or burrows, or creep slowly from place to place, or scamper along over wide areas.

The Pyramid of Food

The sea maintains a delicate balance of all living forms. Each group has a place on the ladder of life, devouring others to keep alive so that it, in turn, can serve as a source of food. Only the mightiest rulers

Many variety of corals grow on the sandy, shallow marine floor of the eastern Caribbean.

Courtesy L. S. Land, Discovery Bay Marine Laboratory, Jamaica, West Indies

A stingray (about 2 feet wide) glides along over a sea of staghorn corals in some 60 feet of water.

Courtesy L. S. Land, Discovery Bay Marine Laboratory, Jamaica, West Indies

of the sea escape this fate. Literally billions of single-celled plants and animals, too tiny or weak to move except as willed by currents and tides, form the base of the food chain. They are called *plankton,* a word chosen because it means *to wander.*

The chain begins when plant plankton convert the energy of sunlight into the basic food supply for all animal life in the seas. Plant plankton, like all plants, depend on sunlight and are therefore generally confined to the upper 300 feet or so of the oceans. Most important of these tiny specks that float about are the single-celled algae, called *diatoms.* Microscopic study reveals their delicate shells — a miniature display of highly decorated beads, needles, chains and triangles. The plankton remove minerals from the seawater to form these intricate houses. Upon death, many shells sink to form the fine, muddy ooze blanketing segments of the ocean bottom.

Animal plankton are the next link in the chain of life. They feed on the plant plankton, consuming them in staggering numbers. The heartiest eaters are the *copepods* with some 750 species, mostly

Courtesy Oceanographer of the Navy

Scientist examines plankton net before it is lowered over the side of an oceanographic research ship.

The killer whale, which is a large porpoise, is a mammal—not a fish. Its peglike teeth are shown here as the whale surfaces.

Courtesy National Oceanic and Atmospheric Administration

the size of a pinhead or a bit larger. Biologists say more copepods fill the oceans than all the ants, bees, butterflies, fish, monkeys, people, and all other multicellular animals in the world combined. A single copepod may eat more than 100,000 diatoms in one day.

Free swimming animals, called *nekton,* feed on the plankton — and on each other. Fish are the most abundant nekton with more than 20,000 species. From the biggest sharks and whales to the tiniest minnows, fish and aquatic mammals gulp down the plankton and the plankton eaters. A single herring may have several thousand copepods in its stomach. Tons of herring are then required to satisfy a hungry fish-eating whale. It is easy to see how billions of plankton are needed to keep up this feeding cycle.

Bottom dwelling animals are known as *benthos* from the Greek word for deep sea. They feed by filtering plankton or organic debris

43

from the seawater or by scavenging the rain of organic matter from life above, or by grazing on plants or eating other animals. Some bottom dwellers, like clams and worms, burrow into the soft mud and sand, while echinoids, snails, and starfish creep along. Barnacles, corals, and oysters all attach to the bottom, spending their entire adult life in one location. In contrast crayfish, crabs, and lobsters move with some speed and agility.

Only flesh-eating creatures inhabit the abyss of the oceans, for plants do not exist there. Many appear like mythological beasts, seeming to be all head and jaws. Monsters indeed, but they are little monsters, generally a few inches to less than a foot in length, for food is too scarce for many large animals to survive.

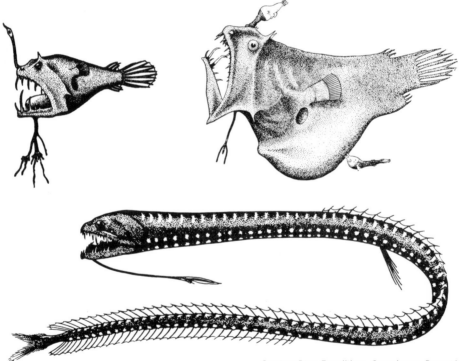

Courtesy Dana Expeditions, Copenhagen, Denmark

Miniature monsters inhabit the ocean depths. Above shows deep-sea anglers, detailing the enormous sizes of the head and mouth. A permanently attached male is on the belly of the female angler at right. Both anglers are only about 2½ to 3 inches long. A fish with spots that glow in the dark is shown below. It is about 6 inches long.

44

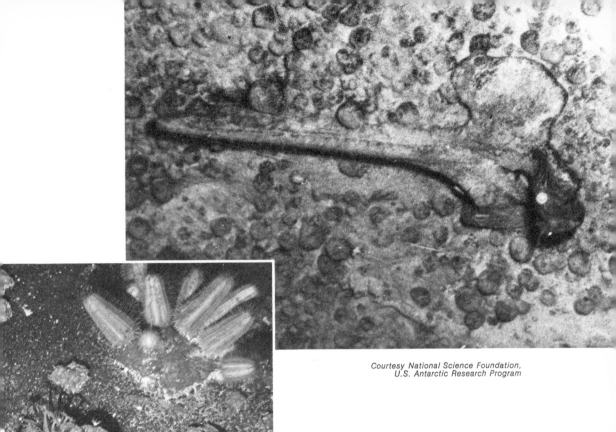

Courtesy National Science Foundation,
U.S. Antarctic Research Program

Rare photographs showing: Above, whale bone on the floor of the Tasmanian Sea (depth 12,840 feet), and left, cactus-like urchin and coelenterata on a peak of the Chile ridge in the southern Pacific (depth 1,260 feet).

Some deep-sea fish create their own light. This luminescence — produced by chemical substances within the body — gives these creatures an eerie glow. Long tails and odd appendages add to the bizarre nature of their bodies. In the eternal darkness of the deep they move blindly in search of food, attacking whatever crosses their path. Large hinging jaws allow their mouths to open wide, and razor-sharp teeth permit a ferocious bite. The oversized mouths enable these creatures to swallow their victims whole, gulping them down quickly. It is no wonder they are known by such names as hatchetfish, dragonfish, gulpers, rattails, and viperfish.

The abundance of life in the seas yields great amounts of waste materials and dead organisms. Most of the dead organisms are quickly

45

eaten by other animals, and the rest decay as marine bacteria return their nutrients to seawater. Rising currents bring these nutrients to the surface where plankton and other marine plants use them for food. Animal waste materials are released directly into the seawater, where they are reutilized by plants. Thus nutrients are cycled and recycled throughout numerous marine food chains.

A Struggle for Survival

Someone has figured that of all the creatures in the oceans, all but one in about 10 million meet a violent death. Many die young and few live to reach maturity. During one spawning period, a single oyster may lay more than 100,000,000 eggs, a cod some 4,000,000. Of these, a few individuals survive to reproductive maturity — and they, in turn, must have enormous spawns to give a few of their offspring a chance for survival. Such is the ruthlessness of the sea!

Man's most dangerous sea enemies are sharks. Over thirty of the many types have been called *man-eaters*. Barely a year goes by without a report of one or more swimmers being attacked by a shark while enjoying the shoreline surf. Sharks are fearless hunters of other free-swimming forms as they continually search for food in the open seas. A few species have earned their killer reputation, however, because of the frenzied way they attack a wounded victim.

Not all predators that signal death to other life in the sea are armed with strong jaws and a full set of sharp teeth, for danger comes in many shapes and sizes. Jellyfish and the Portuguese man-of-war have long tentacles hanging downward innocently from their soft, floating bodies. Yet the stinging cells they contain may kill fish as big as the tentacled drifters themselves.

Some sea anemones attached to the ocean floor wave an attractive array of fleshy tentacles that look like the petals of a colorful flower. An unwary fish cruising by may swim too close. In an instant he is

Danger may lurk near the beautiful plant-like animals of the sea. Left is a sea cucumber and right is a sea anemone protecting a fish that finds its home among the tentacles.

paralyzed by the thousands of needles covering the tentacles. The fish is then swallowed whole by the sea anemone.

Just like the walking stick and the chameleon on land, many creatures of the sea use camouflage to avoid detection or to catch unwary prey. Marine organisms include a remarkable variety of forms that blend into their natural surroundings and wait patiently for their unsuspecting victims. Life in the oceans is a continual struggle for survival — searching for food and attempting to avoid being eaten.

Man accepts this struggle of life in the sea for it is nature's way of avoiding overpopulation. Occasionally, however, catastrophe strikes when nature's balance appears to be upset. So it is with some of the beautiful coral reefs in the Pacific Ocean. Most spectacular of these is the Great Barrier Reef of Australia, a 1,260-mile-long majestic shelf many millions of years in the making. This natural wonder is a crowded complex of marine life.

Prime builders of reefs are corals. Growing in a colony of pouch-like forms, each topped by a ring of flexible tentacles, these brightly-colored animals look much like a cluster of flowering cactus. Minute

47

algae live in close association with the corals. The algae convert sunlight to oxygen and energy-giving nutrients for the corals, which in turn provide protection and nutrient wastes. The growing corals secrete a skeleton of limestone (calcium carbonate) from minerals obtained in the seawater. On this foundation of coral skeletons, a host of other life thrives as the corals continue constructing the reef in the shallow, warm, tropical waters.

A mysterious increase in the numbers of the crown-of-thorns starfish known as *Acanthaster* could spell doom for coral reefs. The bizarre red and green, 16-armed *Acanthaster* now swarms over some Pacific coral reefs in large herds. It exhibits a huge appetite for living coral and has killed vast expanses of the beautiful coral gardens. Their devastation turns the underwater world of pastel colors into a drab graveyard, literally barren of the myriad of reef creatures that once thived there.

Coral gardens are a major tourist attraction to Australia and numerous islands of the Pacific. Even more important, islanders depend upon

The shallow coastal waters off Jamaica show a dazzling array of corals, the main reef-building animals of the seas.

Courtesy L. S. Land, Discovery Bay Marine Laboratory, Jamaica, West Indies

Crown-of-Thorns starfish, *Acanthaster,* moving across a coral reef off the island of Guam in the South Pacific. The white patch is coral, freshly killed by the advancing herd of feeding starfish.

fishing for most of the protein in their diets. When the corals die, many varieties of fish leave the environment. Reefs also act as a protective barrier to the coastline against the erosive attack of storm waves.

Scientists from the United States and Australia, supported by their governments, are now investigating the problem. But even as study is taking place, the relentless coral predators are devouring tracts of valuable Pacific real estate. What caused the present explosion in numbers of the *Acanthaster* and man's possible role in this population imbalance are unanswered questions. Or are such enormous population explosions by *Acanthaster* a bizarre, but normal, part of community life on Pacific coral reefs? The *Acanthaster* problem may not vanish as quickly or as quietly as it developed. But a solution is important because man cannot wait another 50 million years for new reefs to grow.

Courtesy Westinghouse Ocean Research Laboratory

This trained scuba diver injects a Crown-of-Thorns starfish in an effort to kill off the starfish that destroy the reefs.

Lessons from the Sea

Communication systems of dolphins and whales have taught man much about seeing with sound. One study showed that whales talk to each other by a complex pattern of chirps, squeals and whistles. It is possible to determine which whale is speaking by the differences in their voices. Dolphins send out a variety of clicking sounds in a scanning motion. The arrival time and strength of the echoes accurately locate objects, allowing them to detect enemies by a system far superior to the sonar apparatus used on the most modern submarines. Some experts believe dolphins are the most intelligent animals in the sea. Perhaps by a man-dolphin communication system, these marine mammals will be used in undersea rescues and other underwater operations.

Marine life may offer mankind answers to important medical questions too. One such case is a certain type of coelenterate, a pale green fernlike creature which can destroy the virus of the serious liver disease called hepatitis. By learning the secret of how the virus is killed, man may develop a cure or even a way to prevent this illness in humans.

Dogfish sharks offer medicine another fascinating challenge. Normally this shark has a fatty liver, much like a diseased liver in a human being. But when the dogfish shark is placed in fresh water, its liver changes dramatically, and the flow of certain body fluids increases. The liver loses fatty tissue and becomes very similar to a healthy human liver. The key to serious liver ailments which plague mankind may lie in the nature of the body fluids the dogfish shark produces.

A mid-water trawl is lowered from a Navy oceanographic research vessel to catch specimens of the sea life living below the surface zone.

Courtesy Oceanographer of the Navy

Problems in the human nervous system may also be solved by studies of marine animals. The sea hare (a type of snail without a shell) has an extremely simple brain and related nervous system. Understanding precisely how they function may help doctors control nervous disorders in man.

Microscopic, one-celled plants called *dinoflagellates* may even serve humanity. Some varieties are highly toxic and occasionally they

An oceanographer examines a Jamaican coral reef. She carries a pick and sampling bucket to collect specimens and wears a depth gage on her wrist.

Courtesy L. S. Land, Discovery Bay Marine Laboratory, Jamaica, West Indies

"bloom" with a spectacular population explosion. When this happens shorelines are littered with millions of fish which eat these plants and fall victim to the poison. Curiously, however, shellfish consume these plants unharmed for they store the poison in one of their organs. If man eats one of these shellfish which is normally a tasty treat, he becomes seriously ill. The nervous system is affected and paralysis commonly results. Doctors realize that study of the poison in these tiny plants may help man to conquer problems of nerve paralysis.

Sea life may also hold the clue to extracting valuable minerals from seawater. Many elements occur in exceedingly minor amounts in the oceans — in such small quantity, in fact, that they do not show up in chemical tests. Yet some marine organisms are able to store concentrations of these elements in their bodies. The secret of how animals selectively remove certain solid materials from seawater is of great importance. If a similar process could be used on large amounts of seawater, a variety of very useful minerals could be obtained by man.

6

The Land Beneath the Sea

A major discovery was about to take place. It was aboard the H.M.S. *Cook* and the year was 1962. While cruising off the Philippines, the ship passed over a giant gash in the sea floor known as the Mindanao Trench. Even though the oceanographic crew couldn't see to the bottom, they watched with fascination as a record depth of 37,782 feet was recorded by an electronic eye.

Seeing to the ocean bottom is done by sending sound impulses to bounce off the floor and return to the ship. Special receivers called hydrophones pick up each echo signal and record its exact time of arrival. Knowing the speed of sound through seawater and the time required for each electronically controlled sound impulse to reach bottom and return, the water depth is quickly determined.

A continuous series of pulses can be sent out as the ship moves along. As each echo is received, a record of the depth is plotted on a graph. Known as an *echogram,* this graph shows the true shape of the sea floor. In this way an accurate outline of the bottom can be obtained along the ship's path. By criss-crossing the oceans, the shape of the entire sea floor can be pictured.

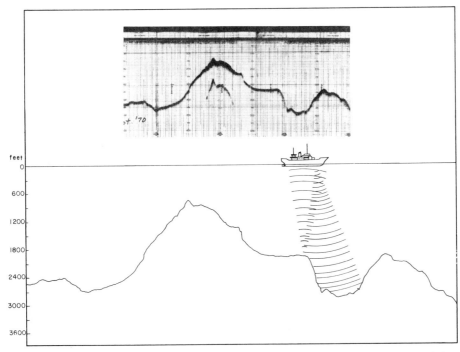

An echogram taken in the northeast Indian Ocean near Sumatra. Depth figures on graph are in fathoms (one fathom equals six feet).

Using echo sounding, oceanographers have discovered a dazzling array of spectacular landforms previously unknown in the darkness of the deep waters. Gaping canyons, some that would nearly span the United States, are many times deeper than the Grand Canyon. Rolling back the ocean waters, one would see jagged mountain ranges extending around the world and lofty volcanic peaks dotting remarkably flat plains that form parts of the sea floor. Earth's underwater landscape is truly an awe-inspiring scene.

Buried Edges of the Continents

The sea washes onto the gently-sloping margins of the land. Called the *continental shelf,* this drowned borderland is the meeting place of land and sea — a dynamic zone of currents, tides, waves, and shifting sediments. The shelf is alive, literally teeming with plants and animals,

55

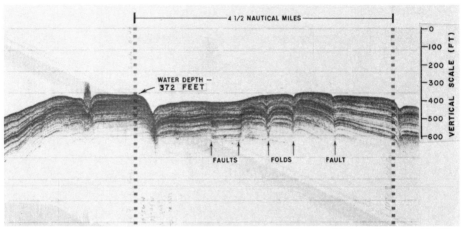

Courtesy U.S. Naval Oceanographic Office

Profile of a segment of the Gulf of Mexico sea floor. Sediment layers reveal their pattern by reflecting seismic waves generated on ship.

for it is the spawning ground of many marine organisms and the birth-place of petroleum.

These underwater terraces act as the land's new blood, for here is where the continents grow. Bits and pieces of rock are carried by rivers and streams as the land mass ever so slowly wears down. The sediments and dead organisms of the shelves then pile up as huge aprons beyond the border of the sea. Coral reefs, rising salt bodies, and other projections may act as dams, allowing the sedimentary wedges to grow behind them. The tiny marine animals and plants that died and were buried in the sediments gradually decay. Through increased heat and pressure with burial, the decayed organic matter slowly converts into substances rich in the elements *hydrogen* and *carbon*. These *hydrocarbons* are known as oil and gas.

A great wall of salt marks the shelf edge for much of the Gulf of Mexico along Texas and Louisiana. In contrast, coral reefs border Florida and form a living shelf in the Florida Keys. Still other coasts like those of states bordering the Pacific Ocean are so young that wide platforms have not had time to develop.

56

Fluctuating sea level also affects the shelves. During the Great Ice Age large volumes of water shifted from the oceans to ice on land. Growth of the continental glaciers was slow, beginning some 2.5 million years ago. During colder intervals, pulses of ice crept southward, buried Canada, and invaded the United States. Finally, gradual warming began about 25,000 years ago, and today only a bit of ice remains on high mountains and in the polar regions of the world. The scars of the ice still exist on the continental shelves. Sea level around the world fell more than 300 feet during the Ice Age. Major segments of the land margins were then exposed and eroded, to modify the gently sloping shelves.

Boundary Walls of the Oceans

Water averages a depth of 430 feet at the outer margin of the continental shelf. Seaward lies the highest, longest, and straightest bluff on earth — the *continental slope* — which plunges two or three miles onto the ocean floor. The slope is even more impressive where young and rugged mountains hug the coastline. For example, the Andes of South America plummet into the Pacific Ocean in a remarkable drop of nine miles from highest mountain peaks to the abyss of the deep.

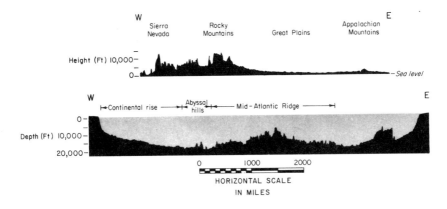

Mountainous features of the Atlantic sea floor compared with the landforms of the United States.

Panoramic view (with fish-eye lens on camera) of small canyon between coral growths at Rio Beno, Jamaica. The sediment flow is heading toward viewer with 40-foot drop-off in the foreground.

Spectacular V-shaped winding canyons are carved into the face of the continental slopes. Imagine a Grand Canyon of the Colorado knifed into the submerged wall of our continent! Such is Monterey Canyon off the California Coast. This twisting gorge, flanked by walls 6000 feet high and 10 miles wide, travels 100 miles down the slope. Another is Hudson Canyon off the eastern coast. A path of currents can be traced from the Hudson River across the continental shelf and into this chasm.

Origin of the submarine canyons remains something of a mystery. A clue was found when oceanographers entered canyons in deep sea submersibles. They noted that at times streams of sediment-rich water pour over the shelf edge and funnel into the canyons. Perhaps the sediments scour the valley walls as they cascade down the slopes.

Triggered by earthquakes or storm agitation along the shorelines, clouds of these sandy waters flush the shelf surface on their journey toward deeper water. An earthquake on November 18, 1929, prompted muddy torrents to flow off the Grand Banks along the southeast coast of Newfoundland. Moving at speeds up to tens of feet per second, these

58

undersea avalanches swept along with enough force to snap a series of trans-Atlantic telegraph cables stretched along the ocean floor. The time at which each successive cable broke provided a record of the velocity and power of the flow. The last cable, some 300 miles offshore, broke thirteen hours after the tremor released the muddy slides.

The Deep Ocean Domain

The shelves and slopes belong to the continents though claimed by water. The sea floor is a world apart, unlike any known on earth or other planets, and it is the unique property of the oceans. Here lies the last earthly domain to be conquered by man, buried under a thick water blanket and hostile to all but a few strange creatures.

Should the seas miraculously disappear tomorrow, a traveler across the ocean basin would find himself gazing at an incredibly strange and foreign land. A vast network of broad sediment fans merge to form the *continental rise.* The rise tapers off the slopes and extends seaward onto

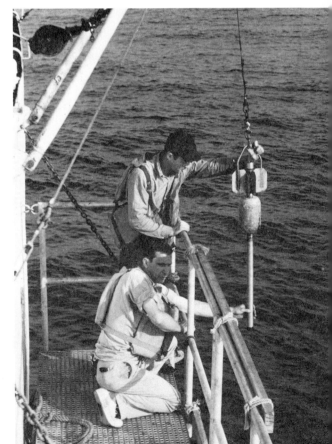

A bottom corer begins its journey to the sea floor where it will plunge into the sediment.

Courtesy National Oceanic and Atmospheric Administration

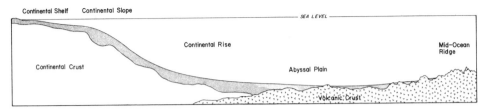

Sketch of sea floor from the continental edge to the mid-ocean ridge.

the sea floor. Here lie the *abyssal plains,* majestic in their flatness, for they are the smoothest surfaces on earth. They occur in patches, interrupted by a scattering of low, oval-shaped hills. Most likely the abyssal hills are higher knolls on the buried irregular topography of the sea floor. The plains are a veneer of fine muds obtained from the seaward tongue of sediment flows which began along the coastlines. Only the hills remain to poke through the blanket, and they, too, are slowly being buried over millions of years by the delicate sheets of fine sediments.

Here and there isolated peaks, sometimes in clusters or rows, tower over their neighbors. Called *seamounts,* about a thousand of these undersea volcanoes are known to rise more than 3,000 feet above the sea floor. Occasionally they break through the water cover into the atmosphere, as with the volcanic chain of the Hawaiian Islands.

Some of these volcanoes are peculiarly flat-topped. Known as *guyots* (pronounced ghee'-ohs), they apparently lost their tops from the cutting edge of breakers and surf when they were near sea level. Since then, perhaps in response to adjustments of the sea floor, they have partially sunk back into the oceans from which they arose. Oceanographers now find these curiously beheaded cones at different depths below the surface of the seas.

Striking, too, are the prominent slashes that mar segments of the ocean floor. These V-shaped cuts are the deepest spots on earth, for in places they drop some seven miles below sea level. A series of these *ocean trenches* ring the Pacific. They commonly occur in bow-like shape, closely paralleling chains of volcanic islands.

Dominating all features is the backbone of the sea floor — a series of ragged hills, the *mid-ocean ridges,* that creep along the ocean basins. This spine of the sea extends as a continuous mountain range through all the oceans around the world. In some places, it forms a low, broad ridge nearly 1,000 miles wide, while it narrows markedly elsewhere. Peaks rising a mile or more above the ridge pierce the water surface to form islands such as the Azores, Ascension, and Tristan de Cunha in the middle of the Atlantic Ocean.

The ridges are even more distinctive because of a prominent gash down their middle. This central rift valley is a narrow, steep-walled notch a mile deep in places. It appears to break the mid-ocean ridges, and even the ocean basins themselves, into separate segments.

The rift valleys are major cracks into the shell of the earth from which molten lava pours from time to time. As the lava hardens, it

An oceanographer slices a core taken from the foothills of the Barbados Ridge of western Atlantic. The core will be checked for tiny fossils on Project GOFAR (Global Ocean Floor Analysis of Research).

Courtesy U.S. Naval Oceanographic Office

forms the dark-colored volcanic rock called basalt. Gradually piled up in this manner, volcanic rock has created the mid-ocean ridges.

Since August, 1968, a unique research ship has zigzagged across the oceans, drilling into the deep-sea floor. The *Glomar Challenger* has made more than thirty cruises, probing sediment layers and volcanic rocks which tell the ancient history of the oceans. A secret to drilling in water up to 20,000 feet deep is to keep the ship steady over one location. At each drill site, the *Glomar Challenger* uses computers to automatically position the ship from signals off a beacon lowered to the ocean floor.

Cores of the ocean floor are the prize of this deep sea drilling project. Once on deck, each core is split in half. One part is refrigerated for future use in a research laboratory and the other half is examined on ship. New prospects for oil in the deep ocean are one important finding from these cores. To date, perhaps the most startling thing *Glomar Challenger* scientists have discovered about the sea floors and

Glomar Challenger, a 400-foot-long vessel, is the first of the heavy ships built for drilling in the open ocean. This drilling derrick stands 194 feet above the waterline.

Courtesy Scripps Institution of Oceanography

Deck of modern, deep-sea drilling ship showing rig in operation.

This drawing shows how a ship remains on station during deep ocean drilling. Sound beacons on the sea floor send pulses to the ship where computer units automatically adjust the ship's position. The drill string is flexible and weighs 400,000 pounds at a water depth of 20,000 feet.

their sediments is that they are much younger than the continents. Realizing this has led to the search for new understanding, not only of the oceans, but of the earth itself.

7

Spreading Seas and Drifting Continents

How often we have all heard the saying, "As solid as a rock!" Are the continents we live on really stable, or are they like icebergs being carried along in a current?

Oceanographers tell us that the mighty Pacific Ocean may be doomed because it is being swallowed as the Americas drift westward. Movements are pitifully slow, however, measured in just a few inches per year. At that rate, many millions of years will pass before lands on opposite sides of the Pacific touch — if they ever do.

On the other side of our continent, the Atlantic Ocean is gradually getting bigger. This means that each year New York and Paris are a little bit farther apart. How long will the Atlantic Ocean continue to grow and what causes this to happen?

Continents Splitting Apart

The idea that the continents once fit together like pieces of a giant jigsaw puzzle is not new. The remarkable similarity of the coastline shapes on either side of the Atlantic triggered the theory that these continents were once joined. In 1912, a German meteorologist named Alfred Wegener suggested that at one time all land masses on earth formed a single, massive supercontinent called *Pangaea.* Then some

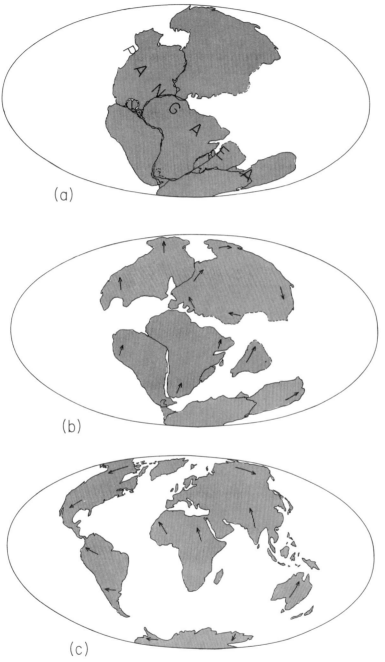

Courtesy Dietz and Holden, Scientific American, 1970

Some 200 million years ago Pangaea may have looked like the top diagram (A). The break-up of the continents after perhaps 65 million years of drift is shown in the middle diagram (B). The drift continued until the present (C).

200,000,000 years ago Pangaea broke apart and the continents we know today began to drift to their present positions.

For nearly fifty years scientists argued about Wegener's idea, some calling it clearly outrageous. In the 1950's, however, new life was added to his theory through study of the ocean floors.

This rebirth began when scientists found that some rocks show *paleomagnetism,* a kind of fossil magnetism. This feature occurs because certain minerals contain abundant iron and are attracted to a magnet. The iron-rich mineral "magnetite" gets its name because it is strongly magnetic. As these minerals form, for example in lava cooled from the eruption of a volcano, the magnetite crystals line up with the earth's magnetic field as if they were tiny compass needles. Like fossils imbedded in the rocks, these magnetic minerals are a permanent record of the earth's magnetic field of the past.

Curiously, magnetic patterns found in many older rocks on different continents don't match those of the earth's present magnetic field. This tells us that the position of the magnetic field has not always remained the same. It appears that the magnetic poles of the earth have gradually shifted their position. Hundreds of millions of years ago, the north magnetic pole was in the middle of the Pacific Ocean, and it has since wandered across Japan and Siberia before reaching its present location.

Stranger yet are the results when paleomagnetism in rocks from different continents is compared. The path of polar wandering determined from North America does not match the path plotted from rocks in Europe. Indeed, the continents themselves must have moved with respect to each other to get these different paths.

Moving Segments of the Ocean Floor

The secret of *how* continents move lies in the mid-ocean ridges. Oceanographers believe these ridges mark giant cracks where spreading

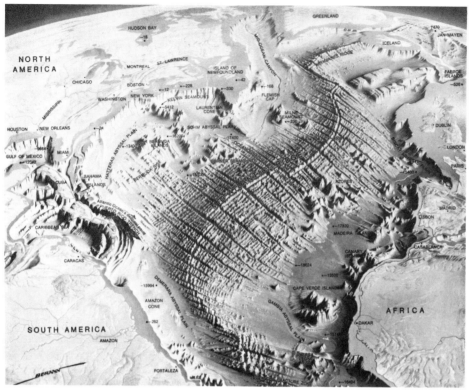

Mountainous features of the Atlantic sea floor compared with the landforms of the United States.

of the sea floor takes place. Earth's interior is hotter than its crust. This increase in temperature downward causes heated material within the earth to rise, just like heated smoky air in a chimney. Molten rock from the earth's interior approaches the surface below the ocean ridges. The ocean floor splits apart along deep rifts that form in the ridge centers as the lava spews out.

The spreading ocean-floor material must go somewhere so it moves sideways in segments, called *plates,* ramming against the continents. In this way continental blocks are rafted along, sometimes riding up and over the sea floor, other times buckling against the oceanic plates.

Each time the sea floor spreads to make room for lava welling up, a bit more of the ocean edge disappears. Oceans, then, grow along the middle and their oldest parts can be found on the margins. Age patterns of the sea floor support this view. These ages are determined from the fossils found within the sediments blanketing the ocean bottom. The youngest sediment covers the central part of each ridge and older sediment is found off the ridge flanks and on the abyssal plains. This spreading mechanism therefore explains why the oceans are so very young compared with rocks many millions of years older found on the continents.

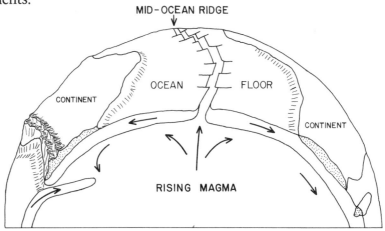

This sketch shows the spreading ocean floor which causes drifting of the continents.

A peculiarity of the earth's magnetic field gives further proof that the oceans spread apart along the ridges. Investigating changes in magnetic patterns in rocks led to a curious discovery. In some samples the position of the north magnetic pole was totally reversed. The south magnetic pole was in its place! The cause of the "flip" of the magnetic poles remains something of a mystery, but it has taken place — not once, but many times during the past hundred million years.

Magnetic reversals in the volcanic rocks of the ocean ridges provide a test for sea-floor spreading. A part of the ridge in the Indian Ocean was chosen for this test during the year 1963. A *magnetometer* (an instrument which measures the strength of magnetic attraction) was towed behind a ship crossing the Indian Ridge. Readings alternated — some registered strongly magnetic while others recorded much weaker

A new crust of the earth is shown welling onto the crest of the South Pacific
Ocean ridge. This photograph was
taken during a cruise of the USNS *Eltanin* at a depth of about 10,250 feet.

values. Several more trips across the ridge at different latitudes gave
similar results. The magnetic patterns formed alternately strong and
weak bands parallel to the ridge crest.

Quite possibly, oceanographers agreed, the bands of strong magnetism occurred over rocks that contained "normal" polarity (north
magnetic pole in the same hemisphere as found today) and weak magnetism existed where the polarity was reversed. One further feature remained to be checked. If the oceans do split and spread along the central
rift of the ridge, the magnetic patterns on opposite sides of the crest
would be identical. Ship surveys on opposite flanks of the ridge proved
this to be true. Bands on one side of the ridge were a mirror image of
the other.

Earthquakes and Volcanoes: Signals of Internal Unrest

Suddenly one afternoon in the summer of the year 79, A.D., a
sleeping volcano erupted. Italy's Mount Vesuvius belched forth lava
burying the city of Pompeii and its 20,000 inhabitants beneath fifteen

69

A volcanic island named Surtsey rises out of the North Atlantic off the coast of Iceland as lava erupts on the mid-Atlantic ridge.

to twenty-five feet of volcanic debris. Even today, nearly 2000 years later, the threat of Vesuvius looms great, for it has erupted some seventy times during recorded history. What is happening within the earth's crust to create Mount Vesuvius and keep it active for so many years?

Volcanoes occur in clusters such as the one including Mount Vesu-

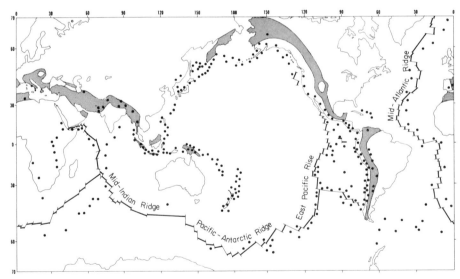

Pattern of ridges in the oceans. Volcanoes (shown by dots) ring the Pacific and follow the ridges. Recent mountain ranges (shaded areas) along the western edge of the Americas and across the southern edge of Eurasia mark the zones where segments of sea floor and continent collide.

vius along the edge of the Mediterranean Sea. The "Ring of Fire" bordering the Pacific Ocean is another famous belt of volcanoes. Earthquakes, too, occur in clusters, generally in the same areas as volcanoes. This is not surprising because earthquakes normally accompany the eruption of a volcano.

Spreading of the ocean floors explains why volcanoes and earthquakes occur in clusters and what happens within the crust to cause them. As oceanic material is shoved against and under the continental edges, crinkling and folding of the rocks takes place. Periodically, abrupt movements of the rocks result in earthquakes and the release of molten material from deeper crustal zones. The Ring of Fire marks the zone where Pacific Ocean material is being rammed under the continents along its borders.

The Mediterranean Sea — A Former Ocean?

A clue as to why Mount Vesuvius and other volcanoes border Italy may be found in the *Tethys Sea*, ancestor to our modern Mediterranean. Perhaps the greatest seaway of all time, the Tethys extended in an east-west trend along the northern side of the present-day lands of Africa, Arabia and India. No one knows exactly when the Tethys came into existence, but its birth was probably some 400 million years ago. It formed a gigantic body more than 1000 miles wide separating the southern hemisphere from Europe and Asia to the north.

For many millions of years, huge amounts of sediments were dumped into this oceanic trough by rivers flowing off the continents bordering the Tethys. Then, ever so slowly, the land masses from north and south moved toward each other. As the Tethys Sea closed, these approaching continents acted as a gigantic vise, compressing millions of cubic feet of the sediments in the narrowing ocean trough. Slowly these sediments, which had been hidden by the water, were squeezed upward. Gradually, over some 200 million years, they rose to form mountains along the edges of the sea.

Along most of its former length, evidence of the Tethys Sea has disappeared completely. Arabia and India are crunched against Asia with the lofty Himalayan Mountains standing where the deep sea once existed. The Himalayas are joined to the west by the rugged Alpine chain which bounds the northern side of the Mediterranean. The once great Tethys was thus reduced to the Mediterranean Sea we know today.

Like the ocean waters, the present ocean basins differ from those of the past. Such differences in shape can only mean that the continents themselves have moved about through geologic time — and perhaps changed in size — in response to what has happened beneath the earth's crust.

Oceanographers prepare to lower a trawl over side of their ship. The trawl is dragged behind the ship to collect specimens from the sea floor.

Courtesy Oceanographer of the Navy

Oceanographers have come to realize that answers to these mysteries of the land lie deep within the earth. Changes on the surface of the globe may be a result of its gradual increase in size. Perhaps the planet earth has been expanding over millions of years — like a balloon being slowly blown up. Even more likely, the earth's crustal skin has slipped about over the heated interior. Due to this slippage the continents could have changed their shapes and positions even if the globe has remained a constant size. Some scientists think both processes have occurred.

The Oceans Today

No one really knows how many oceans have come and gone in the ages past, but our present world of water has three great oceans — the Atlantic, Indian, and largest of them all, the Pacific. They are really parts of one continuous body for they join "at the bottom of the world." There they form the Antarctic Ocean which circles the continent of Antarctica. They meet again at the ice-covered North Pole as the Arctic Ocean.

Scientists have proved that our present ocean basins are distinct from those of eons ago, and probably from those in ages to come. To be sure, the ocean waters are more stable than the containers they fill, for ours is a dynamic planet, composed of drifting continents and moving ocean floors. Scientists believe that earth's surface will continue to be dominated by water.

8

Shorelines: Harbors of Life and Rivers of Sand

Powerful tides from the Pacific Ocean surge through the Golden Gate and into San Francisco Bay twice each day. On the landward side, the Sacramento and San Joaquin Rivers flow over a segment of the continent and then pour into the bay. Fresh and salt water mix in an enormous circulation system as vital to marine life as blood is to the human body. Bays and estuaries are unique, for they represent the partly enclosed portions of the oceans where sea meets land. Here exist the spawning grounds of much life important to food chains throughout the oceans.

A wealth of living creatures inhabits the shoreline and coastal shelf, basking in the sunlight which extends to the shallow sea floor. The population is sometimes so great that finding a place to settle on the bottom may be a difficult task for sea anemone or brittle star. There the animals scour the sea floor or lift bright tentacles aloft to catch the rain of bountiful food. Yet amidst the plenty there is danger, for this population can survive only if conditions of sea temperature, salinity, and sediment content remain within certain limits. Man and nature can upset this delicate balance.

Oxygen is a key ingredient, essential to the vitality of these shoreline water bodies. San Francisco Bay is a good example. A normal balance

Courtesy L. S. Land, Discovery Bay Marine Laboratory, Jamaica, West Indies

An abundance and variety of life thrives along the shallow north shore of Jamaica. Staghorn corals (in the foreground) are common.

of life can exist only if oxygen is in ample supply, for it is necessary for plant and animal respiration, and in the chemical alteration of organic matter. Marsh grasses and underwater plants furnish oxygen to the bay waters, but man has filled the mudflats and constructed high-rise apartments where once water lapped over thriving plant life in the tidelands. This intrusion reduces the source of oxygen. Furthermore, sewage and other city wastes dumped into the bay use up oxygen as they decompose. So, as oxygen in the water becomes less and less, life in San Francisco Bay struggles to survive.

Each inlet along the coast has a natural "pump" which keeps it clean, removing sewage and other undesired materials. Such is the role of the tides. Their flushing action however, takes time, sometimes years, and man's wastes may be poured in at a faster rate. Groins, jetties and other man-made features slow down the natural water circulation and

75

Sea urchins abound on the coral reef along the north shore of Jamaica.

make the tidal cleansing more difficult. These obstructions accelerate the rate at which bays and inlets become cesspools, unfit for fish and wildlife.

Desire to preserve our coastlines is mounting and, hopefully, the future may not be so grim. In 1969, the California legislature established the Bay Conservation and Development Commission to control bay fill operations in order to prevent their destruction. Numerous other shoreline areas are likewise being studied by states and the federal government. One is Tampa Bay, Florida, where the Tampa Port Authority, aided by government scientists, is striving to make sure that the area's natural resources are not harmed.

Man and the Water's Edge

The sea otter is a playful creature that lives along the California coast, but his valued pelt has made him fair game for hunters. Thousands of sea otters have been killed by fishermen for their hides.

Man's eagerness to catch sea otters created an imbalance of nature. Otters have a tremendous appetite for sea urchins, those spiny creatures that look like a purple pin-cushion with long needles. When many otters had been killed, the urchins thrived. They invaded the underwater forest of their favorite food, the giant kelp, like a plague of grasshoppers. Eating the rootlike bases of the tall strands of this rich submarine jungle, the urchins left a bleak wasteland of rock and sand where once vegetation thrived.

Deprived of food and home, fish and lobsters moved away. The fishing industry became alarmed. Even skin diving was no longer exciting.

In 1971, Project Urchin Review Panel, called PURP, was formed in Los Angeles to solve the problem. Many thousands of divers agreed to scour kelp beds off the beaches and smash the urchins with hammers. That accomplished, they began a long process of kelp bed replanting. The sea otters are now protected but until enough of them come back to keep the urchins in balance, the kelp beds will be threatened.

Duck farming is big business on Long Island, N. Y., where one of every two ducks in the United States is raised each year. Several million ducks produce a lot of raw wastes, and much of it has been

Hordes of sea urchins move along the shallow sea floor near Point Loma, California. They climb the giant kelp, eating the plants at their base.

washed into Great South Bay, causing the water in places to turn a sludgy gray. As the decaying organic matter settles, bottom-dwelling creatures suffocate and the oxygen in the water is greatly reduced.

The Long Island oyster industry has been hard hit by the duck pollution because oysters need clear water to feed. Dirty water clogs their gills and they soon starve or suffocate. As the farming of ducks increased, oyster production fell sharply. In contrast, clams thrived because they are able to feed in these polluted waters. The answer then is simple — dig for clams instead of diving for oysters. Not quite, because some of the clams collect bacteria which are attracted to the duck wastes. If eaten, these contaminated clams can cause severe intestinal infections in man. So even though clams have multiplied, many infected clam beds are now closed and a million-dollar clam industry is threatened.

The growing population on Long Island adds to the problem because some of man's wastes also enter Great South Bay, but a solution can be found. All human sewage should be treated before being released. Duck wastes can be collected, dried, and sold as fertilizer. Money made by fertilizer sales can help to pay waste treatment costs.

Except for some free-swimming forms, the complex life at the ocean's edge is sharply zoned. Plants and animals suited for the splash zone bridge the gap between land and water. Seaward lie three distinct tidal zones, each with its unique community of life.

During periods of extremely low tide — which occur only a few times each month — isolated pools dot California's coastline. The giant green anemone, the sea cucumber, and other exotic creatures which are usually underwater, then lie exposed. Man's fascination for collecting the unusual has led him to the shore during these low tides, and to the rarer shells found in the pools stranded from the retreating water. Perhaps the main attraction has been the edible abalone, a tasty mollusk which has become increasingly hard to find.

An oceanographer wearing scuba gear examines a variety of corals (sea whip in foreground, brain coral behind) found along North Rock, Bermuda. The water depth is approximately 110 feet.

Fortunately, the California Department of Fish and Game recognized the threat to low-tide life forms. In March, 1972, a new regulation went into effect which prohibits collecting them from tidal pools except by written permission. Such permits are generally restricted to scientific collecting.

Oysters present a special problem along the Gulf of Mexico. As a source of food they support an industry of ten million dollars per year. Because oysters can not move, the oyster beds must be protected from contamination. Oyster shell, however, is an important source of building material and provides lime for chemical and cement plants. It is dredged from natural reefs where it accumulates in thick deposits.

Dredging the shell disturbs the living oysters and sometimes the muddy water interferes with their feeding habits. Therefore the oyster farmers are not happy with the shell dredgers. Each industry claims the right to a valuable resource, but the two are in conflict.

79

Management of shoreline resources by state and federal agencies is sometimes required to solve such differences. Restrictions on each industry are necessary to assure that it does not contaminate the environment for others.

Beaches: Sediment on the Move

The beach is a soft sand carpet that marks the edge of the sea. Stretching along the rim of the ocean, it may seem that beaches were placed there solely to serve man's pleasure. The sandy shores of Long Island alone attract some 70 million people each year. Beaches fascinate man for they offer a view of the power and mystery of the oceans. With each wave that crashes on the shore, bits and pieces of an underwater world are spread along the water's edge. But beaches do a great deal more because they protect the land from the fury of the oceans.

Yet, beaches are not permanent. They are really rivers of sand — always moving and forever changing shape. Beaches can even disappear when man foolishly tampers with the supply of their millions of tiny moving pieces. They are but one part of a bigger system of sediment flow. It starts high on the continents where rivers and streams are born and ends at the depths of the seas, off the edges of the continents.

Beaches are made of whatever materials are available to them, generally picked up by rivers as they flow over the land. Tiny chips of rock and grains of resistant minerals are most common, for beaches represent the crumbled remains of former mountains. Added to this are fragments of sea shells broken by waves and currents, and strewn onto the beach.

Waves meet the shore at an angle, and as they wash onto land, a portion of their energy moves water and sediment parallel to the coast. The movement of water along the shore, called *longshore currents,* carries this mixture of rocks, minerals and shells in a zigzag trail along the water's edge.

The amount of sand moved is tremendous. Measurements show that several hundred thousand cubic yards of sediment per year pass any one place on the California coast on the journey southward. Eventually the sand reaches a notch in the coastal shelf and plummets seaward down a submarine canyon to form a huge underwater apron on the deeper ocean floor below.

Man barricades this stream of sand in an effort to satisfy his needs. Dams on the rivers hold back water, but they also halt the flow of sand necessary to nourish the beaches. With many beaches now trapped at the foot of some dam, the search for sand becomes more hectic. Sand is being trucked to Hawaii's famous Waikiki Beach from nearby dunes. In some places, beach owners have even had to make artificial beach sand by crushing up rock chips and gravel.

A series of groins jut out from shore along Miami Beach, Florida, and curb the longshore flow of beach sand.

Once on shore, the tiny grains face obstacles placed there by man. Each groin, jetty and pier obstructs shoreline flow. To be sure, a jetty may build up the beach front of the owner, but perhaps at a cost to his neighbors, for the beach robs sand at one place to feed another. Soon each property is bounded by a wall jutting out to sea, and the motion of longshore currents is greatly hampered. As longshore flow slows down, sand clogs up the inlets to bays, estuaries and lagoons. Man must then remove the sediment fill to keep these inlets open.

The beach alone stands before the mighty waves of a storm-angered sea as it lashes the coast. Nature built the finer sand into dunes behind the beach as an additional barrier to inland flooding. Man has altered this pattern. Constant demand for construction along the shoreline has removed much of the beach. Dune buggies have also done their share, blazing trails over the soft sand and killing vegetation which keeps the dunes from eroding away.

A seawall, man's protection against the erosive power of waves crashing onto the shore, viewed along the Gulf of Mexico at Galveston, Texas. The large rocks at the toe of the seawall reduce the wave action.

Courtesy U.S. Army Coastal Engineering Research Center

Destruction caused by a seismic sea wave which hit the coast of Hawaii in 1960.

When hurricane warnings go out, the bathers leave but the fifteen-story hotels remain. They bear the wrath of a storm meant to beat upon the dunes. It is no wonder that well over 200 million dollars have been spent in the United States in the past twenty years to control beach erosion.

Nature's Own Peril to the Coasts

Without warning, on June 15, 1896, tragedy struck Japan. A great wall of water nearly one hundred feet high crashed onto the shore swallowing everything in its path. When the giant waves passed, the toll was shocking — 27,000 people perished and 10,000 houses were swept into the sea.

Japan had just experienced the devastating effects of seismic sea waves, also known as *tsunamis*. They are commonly called tidal waves, although scientists avoid the name because they are not caused by tides. These mighty waves had their beginning hundreds of miles away when the ocean floor shook under the grasp of an earthquake. An earthquake is the tremor or shaking of the earth which can be felt when a segment of the crust shifts. When an earthquake rocks the sea floor, it may set in motion seismic waves in the water above. Crustal movements near the shoreline can also cause a tsunami by triggering a landslide. A mass of rock sweeps down the continental shelf and is dumped into deeper water causing these waves to form. Either way the result is the same — a tsunami.

Tsunamis may cross open water undetected, but when they "feel bottom" along the coast, they build up to thunderous waves that crash with fury upon the beach. To alert people of pending disaster, the U.S. Coast and Geodetic Survey has developed a Seismic Wave Warning System. When an earthquake is pinpointed, tidal gauges placed throughout the oceans are checked for the first sign of a seismic sea wave passing by. Warnings are then flashed to shore well ahead of the waves. This advance signal allows steps to be taken to protect property along the water's edge and cautions people to head for higher ground.

Tsunamis are not the only natural disaster to hit coastlines. *Hurricanes* are an even greater threat. These whirlwind monsters form a spiral of air spinning around an "eye" of extremely low pressure. Gusts of wind may reach 200 miles per hour or more as the storm picks up size and speed crossing the open waters. Havoc is wreaked by winds and water when the hurricane touches land. Huge waves pile onto the beach and torrential rains beat down upon the coast. Damage is frightening as the storm moves inland until it slowly loses energy and dies — sometimes hundreds of miles from the coast

Hurricanes are born in the tropics as small storms, but under a combination of conditions they may grow to several hundred miles across. Air near the earth's surface feeds a center of low pressure and then rises up a funnel which may reach 10 miles high. Cyclonic winds flow outward from the top, then swoop down. The air warms, picks up moisture, and is sucked back into the hurricane.

Man has "eyes in the sky" watching over him and looking for hurricanes. They are the weather satellites. They orbit the earth daily, relaying photographs to national weather centers. Once a storm is spotted, hurricane hunters go to work. These flying daredevils head directly into the storm to check its air speed, pressure differences, and the overall size of gale-force winds. Close watch is kept on the whirling storm and its path is carefully charted. Coastal alert warns people who live where the hurricane is headed. But watch out! These storms are unpredictable and may shift direction at the last moment.

Project Stormfury is now on the march to destroy hurricanes. Planned jointly by the U.S. Departments of Commerce and Defense, storm seeding is being tested to see if hurricane strength can be substantially reduced. Silver iodide particles are dropped by plane into the clouds ringing the eye of the storm. The idea is to cause ice crystals to

A weather satellite orbiting the earth photographs cloud patterns and reveals five hurricanes. These pictures were taken on September 14, 1967.

Courtesy National Oceanic and Atmospheric Administration

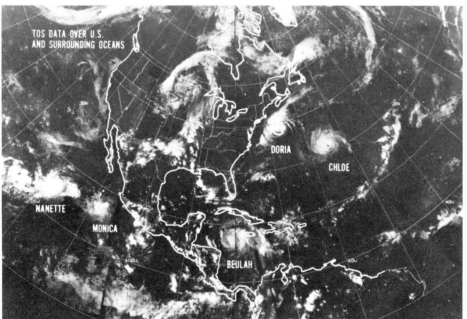

View of Hurricane *Beulah* from ESSA 3 weather satellite on September 16, 1967, as the storm crossed the Gulf of Mexico.

form, removing heat from the main whirling mass. This action spreads energy formerly concentrated in the hurricane center over a wider area and decreases wind speeds. Preliminary tests are encouraging and hurricanes may be on the way to oblivion.

Hurricanes and tsunamis can severely upset nature's balance in bays and estuaries. In its trip up the Atlantic coast in June 1972, Hurricane Agnes dumped heavy rains over the land. Cities and towns along stream banks were flooded, and swollen rivers poured into Chesapeake Bay. Oysters, clams, and crabs were among the sealife in the bay to suffer from an unusual pollutant — too much fresh water. The delicate balance of mixing fresh and sea water had been upset. Some sea life was not able to survive the change. Agnes' deluge also carried tons of raw sewage and pesticide run-off into the bay. Damage to the fishing industry ran into millions of dollars as some favorite food fish became inedible because of the contamination.

Despite the damage, Agnes was a blessing to some oysters and to bathers. These same flood waters flushed out to sea certain shell-boring snails that feed on oysters. Stinging jellyfish were also swept into the Atlantic Ocean, allowing bathers sting-free swimming all summer.

Hurricane *Betsy* brought tragedy to the Louisiana coast in September, 1965. Red.Cross workers reported it was one of the worst storms ever to hit the Gulf Coast of U.S. with 2,600 homes destroyed and 164,000 damaged.

Courtesy National Oceanic and Atmospheric Administration

9

A New Frontier of Treasure

"Let's put the animals of the sea to work," exclaim some scientists who look hopefully to the wealth of minerals dissolved in the ocean waters. The common oyster collects copper at a rate 200 times the amount found in the seawater it filters. Some marine snails store concentrations of iron and lead, and sea squirts have the amazing ability to store the rare element *vanadium* in their bodies at a level 50,000 times that in the seas. Ear bones of whales and shark teeth contain extraordinary amounts of certain minerals. Fluid wastes produced by the octopus have nearly 200 times as much zinc as is found in normal seawater. Perhaps in the future these and other animals will be raised in sea "farms" for the metals they collect.

Valuable Minerals in Solution

Imagine 25 tons of gold in every cubic mile of seawater. This is really not very much compared to the 128 million tons of common salt (sodium chloride) in that same cubic mile of the sea. The oceans contain an abundance of minerals in solution. Man's problem is to find a cheap way to take these minerals from the water.

Chemists and engineers of the Dow Chemical Company paved the way by successfully removing magnesium from seawater. In a series of

The Dow Chemical plant at Freeport, Texas produces one pound of magnesium from each 142 gallons of sea water. Settling ponds, where a mixture of lime and water called "milk of lime" mixes with sea water, are shown in foreground.

chemical processes which includes using lime made from oyster shells, they produced 99.8 percent pure magnesium. Most of the U.S. supply of this important metal now comes from the oceans.

Bromine, too, has been successfully drawn from seawater. Demands for bromine rose sharply in the mid-1920's when cars became popular and it was needed for "anti-knock" gasolines. Scientists turned to bromine in seawater when other sources, like burned seaweed and wells drilled to tap salt-rich water, could not meet the needs. A chemical process for removing bromine was developed in test plants on the Atlantic coast. More than 2,500 gallons of seawater are now treated at these plants to get each pound of bromine. The process is a success and 80 percent of the U.S. supply of bromine for use in dyes, photography, drugs and medicines, as well as in gasoline, now comes from the oceans.

As early as 1000 B.C., the Chinese used salt that they removed from the oceans. Today, however, it is generally cheaper to mine salt than to take it from the sea. Most of the salt currently used for industry and for our food was once dissolved in ocean waters. Salt formed when ancient seas were trapped on land and the water in them dried up. During millions of years since then, the salt deposits have been buried in the earth's crust. And so salt now taken from these mines really comes from the oceans of long ago.

For nearly 100 years man has dreamed of the wealth of the oceans' gold, but as yet no cheap way has been found to remove it from solution. Gold was first extracted from seawater in the mid-1930's, but alas, only a mere speck was obtained from 12 tons of seawater. Perhaps someone will soon find a way to cut the cost of tapping this treasure.

A mineral of greater dollar value is heavy hydrogen, called *deuterium,* which abounds in the oceans. "There is enough deuterium to supply man's energy needs for decades ahead," assert some scientists. Deuterium is needed to operate nuclear fusion power plants of the future. The deuterium in the sea is possibly worth hundreds of millions of dollars. However, a method for controlling fusion in producing energy must be found before the deuterium can be put to use.

Mining the Sea Floor

A monstrous vacuum cleaner creeps along the sea floor, sucking up rock and mud that coats the bottom. Its target — a wealth of potato-like lumps, called nodules, spread over an estimated 14 million square miles of the oceans. These mysterious nodules contain a surprisingly high amount of manganese and some have cobalt, copper, and nickel as a bonus.

Sizes of the nodules vary, but most are a few inches in diameter. Generally black or dark brown, some are soft enough to be cut with a

A vast field of baseball-sized manganese nodules is spread over the deep floor of the south-western Pacific (depth about 17,250 feet). Photographed during cruise of USNS *Eltanin*.

knife. When sliced open, they reveal a pattern of thin layers like that of an onion. Very often the center of the nodule contains small fragments of lava, a lump of clay, or even a shark tooth or other bit of marine skeletal material.

Probably the manganese in the nodule comes largely from undersea volcanic eruptions. Some is brought to the seas by rivers washing over the land. How these nodules form is not entirely known. Apparently fine particles of manganese and iron slowly collect on hard objects lying on the sea floor. Gradually more and more metal is attracted and the nodules continue to grow.

Mining this vast supply of metal-rich nuggets is not an easy venture, for they are spread over wide areas and extend to the deep ocean floor. The most difficult task is to gather the nodules and get them into a ship. Giant suction machines sound simple, but extensive dredging in water 14,000 feet deep has never been done. Perhaps dragline buckets on a conveyor belt from ship to sea bottom will prove more successful.

Time will tell how costly the operation will be and when manganese nodules can be mined more cheaply than deposits on land.

Man also looks to the sea floor for diamonds as well as gold — among earth's most precious treasures. He finds both on the underwater continental edges, especially concentrated in the bottoms of gullies and other buried river channels. The diamonds and gold are carried there by rivers flowing over deposits on land.

One place to look for diamonds is just offshore from the rich diamond mines in Southwest Africa. Here floating diamond diggers such as the prospecting ship, *Rockeater,* patrol the coastline. *Rockeater* was specially designed by Ocean Science and Engineering Company for this task. It can drill to depths of 500 feet and pump the gravel aboard the ship from that depth.

Ships like *Rockeater* resemble floating factories as they crawl along, dredging for buried jewels. Many operate continuously, twenty-four hours a day, seven days a week. On board, rock and sand sucked up

Rockeater, complete with drilling rig for testing diamond-bearing gravels off the coast of Southwest Africa.

Courtesy DeBeers Consolidated Mines Limited

Two styles of drilling rigs in the Gulf of Mexico with helicopter landing platforms. At left is a fixed platform rig 70 miles offshore from Louisiana in 210 feet of water; at right, a self-elevating or jackup rig useful in different water depths.

from the sea floor are washed, screened, and carefully sorted. Then the diamonds are picked out by hand.

Perhaps the famous gold rushes of nearly a century ago may again hit Alaska and the Yukon, but with one slight difference. This time the gold will be undersea, for it has been discovered in the shallow waters off the beaches of Nome, Alaska. The search is also active along the coast of Nova Scotia where gold has been found in offshore gravel deposits.

Surprisingly, the most valuable submarine metal deposits mined are not gold, but tin. For many years tin has been dredged from the waters off Thailand. Extensive tin deposits are believed to exist farther offshore from Thailand and along the Malaysian coastline of the South China Sea.

Riches on the Continental Shelf

A helicopter buzzes along some one hundred miles off the Texas-Louisiana coast. Then its destination looms ahead, a giant steel tower poking out of deep water in the Gulf of Mexico. A "target" marks the landing site for the helicopter, which is bringing men and supplies from land. This is an offshore oil rig, with steel legs firmly planted on the floor of the continental shelf, some 200 feet below. The drilling platform is a combination working area and living quarters. Many of the crew stay aboard weeks at a time as the drilling goes on.

Oil is indeed "black gold" for the amount needed in the United States is fantastic. Every day, 650 million gallons of petroleum (oil that has been processed by refineries) are used in the U.S. alone! As our population increases, demands for more petroleum grow — more homes, bigger industries, greater travel by car and plane. Without oil, and the natural gas which forms with it, this nation could not have developed its world leadership.

Oil and gas lie buried in the rocks under the oceans. Tiny marine plants and animals died and were buried in sediments on the ocean floors many millions of years ago. Gradually this organic matter decayed and changed into substances rich in the elements hydrogen and carbon that form oil and gas.

Since the first oil well was drilled in 1859, man has searched for this hidden treasure. He looked first on land, but by the 1940's oil was found under the shoreline swamps of Louisiana. The next step was the submerged edge of the continent, which is covered by rock layers that contain oil. Rigs to drill in shallow water were designed, then floating platforms moved into deeper water. Now platforms dot the continental shelf off the Gulf of Mexico and ships like *Glomar Challenger* cruise the oceans, drilling in the open seas.

94

World energy needs will demand a rapid expansion in offshore drilling. The rich oil deposits on Alaska's North Slope are now being counted on heavily to help the United States through its energy crisis in the next few years. Oil reserves buried on the world's continental margins are a highly sought treasure, ever more valuable as fuels for energy become scarcer. Controlling the rights to drill in open waters presents additional international problems. Already several countries have staked their claims in the North Sea where valuable oil and gas deposits occur. New concerns about "who owns the oceans" are arising as many nations prepare to drill beyond their coastal waters.

Oil and gas are not the only riches found by drilling into rock layers on the continental shelf. For here and there, rising upward through layers of sediment in the Gulf of Mexico, are domes of salt. They rise,

Artist's conception shows a semi-submersible drilling rig which can be towed into deep water as a floating platform.

Courtesy The Offshore Company

much like bubbles of air released by a SCUBA diver, because the buried salt beds are lighter than the thick piles of sediment dumped on them. The salt flows slowly, over millions years, inching toward the surface. Resting on the crests of many of these domes is a valuable yellow mineral — sulfur!

Courtesy Freeport Minerals Company

The world's first and only offshore sulfur operation is seven miles from the Louisiana coast in the Gulf of Mexico. The melted sulfur is pumped to shore in a pipeline trenched into the floor of the Gulf.

Curiously, sulfur forms by the action of bacteria that live in the rocks containing oil. These bacteria actually change the sulfur ions existing in other minerals into a concentration of relatively pure sulfur. No wonder they are commonly called the "sulfur-loving bacteria."

Sulfur melts at temperatures only slightly hotter than boiling water. For this reason the *Frasch process,* designed by an American chemist named Herman Frasch, is used to remove the sulfur. Three pipes are placed in each drill hole. Superheated water is pumped down one of these pipes into the sulfur body. Compressed air, sent down a second pipe, forces the melted sulfur up the third pipe to the surface. The liquid sulfur is pumped directly into the special pipelines or tankers for transport to shore. It is then ready for industry to use in dyes, matches,

96

Fishing with large nets for menhaden, a type of herring, off the east coast of the U.S.

explosives, paints, paper manufacturing, fertilizers, insecticides, for sulfuric acid and many other purposes.

Our Living Resources: Food from the Sea

Man is a land animal, but the problem of overcrowding might force him to the oceans. He may not live in the oceans but there he will find a variety of marine life for his dinner table. Plankton soup as an appetizer, seaweed in the salad in place of lettuce, and a wide selection of fish and mollusks for the main dish. Even dessert is special, a cake baked with fish flour. The menu may sound strange, but it contains abundant protein as well as vitamins and minerals.

The promise of food from the sea lies in new ways of fishing. From the days of hook and line, the search for marine life has improved to using a variety of fishing nets, called trawls and seines. The fish are netted and hauled aboard modern fishing vessels. Sometimes the catch is huge. Too often, however, fishermen are disappointed. Although fish are plentiful in parts of the oceans, finding them is a persistent problem.

"Tagging" fish has been practiced for years to learn more about their long-range movements. Ingenious methods are now used so fish can even tag themselves. In one system, blue tuna are tagged with baited hooks which break away from the line when the tuna strike, but tagging has not solved the problem, for even though their travel habits are known, schools of fish may still be hard to locate.

Ships commonly use echo sounders to detect schools of nearby fish. Sound waves sent out strike the fish, then return to the ship's recorder. Once located, the crew must catch up with the school and net the fish.

Courtesy National Oceanic and Atmospheric Administration, National Marine Fisheries Service

The shrimp on the conveyor belt are being moved from the trawler to a processing plant. Length measurements of shrimp are important in fishery management.

Imagine, though, a fishing vessel of the future. Specially pitched sounds and bright beacons penetrate the water. As if on command, schools of fish for miles around head for the ship. As they approach, they seek out the probing fingers of long hoses. A slight electric charge surrounds the funnel-like mouth of each hose and lures the fish inside. They are then pumped aboard ship.

98

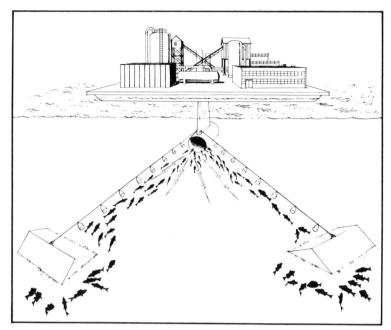

Courtesy National Oceanic and Atmospheric Administration

An underwater fishing platform is being developed at Pascagoula, Mississippi, where underwater lights will attract the fish and an electric field will pull them to an intake.

Unlikely? Not really, for already U.S. fishermen patrol the Atlantic with hoses attached to their nets. Once caught in the net, the fish are pumped through the hose to the ship.

Better ways of hunting fish are only a first step in using ocean life. Man will harvest the crops of marine plants and animals teeming throughout the coastal waters, and eventually, ranch the open seas. Japan has made great strides in harvesting their shorelines and has the most highly developed program of marine aquaculture in the world. On a trip along the Japanese coast one may visit farms where oysters are grown on wooden racks suspended in the water by floats, where prawn (a shellfish much like shrimp) are raised from eggs to market size in a series of feeding ponds, where eel are cultivated, and where shrimp have been hatched and raised for nearly twenty years. The Japanese also breed many varieties of fish to meet their pressing demands for seafood. Even seaweed is cultivated and used in a variety of dishes.

Shrimp ponds on the east coast of Florida near Miami. Shrimp are raised under controlled feeding conditions.

Ranching the open seas will be more difficult. One way is to catch the young fish and transfer them to floating cages. Then by controlled feeding, they can be quickly fattened for market. The Japanese have raised yellow-tail tuna in this way with success. A better method is control of the breeding and growing patterns without having to catch the fish. Large, open-sea pens may be the key. Screens of air bubbles released from submerged hoses may act as "walls" to keep the fish in certain areas — and to keep sharks and other predators out. Once penned in, food can be added to hasten growth of the fish.

Still a great deal of waste occurs in cleaning and butchering fish, and many types of "trash fish" are thrown overboard by commercial fishermen in the daily routine of netting. Fish protein concentrate may be a happy solution to this waste. All the fish and cuttings now discarded can be ground up, treated chemically to remove oils and odor, and dried to powder. This "fish flour" is then ready for cooking and baking. The cost is low and the protein content is high, four times that of fresh fish.

100

Protein is lacking in the diet of people of many nations. Cattle and poultry are too expensive in these countries, so protein from the sea is the hope against starvation.

Oceanographers of the future develop the sea floor resources.

Courtesy National Oceanic and Atmospheric Administration

Skipjack tuna is one of the most important food fish for the U.S. population.

Courtesy National Oceanic and Atmospheric Administration

10

Man and the Oceans

The scene is the sea floor some 8,000 feet below water level: Gliding along at these murky depths is a curious monster. It has six eyes scanning the uneven, sometimes rocky, bottom. It passes a variety of life forms. Brittle stars are scattered here and there on patches of soft mud, and an occasional strange, multicolored fish or octopus swims by. Then one of the monster's robot-like arms reaches out and grabs its prey, dropping it into a special pouch. This arm is guided by a beam of light which radiates from the monster's belly, flooding the darkness of the ocean.

The monster is *Deep Quest,* the special product of research scientists and engineers who have long dreamed that someday man would swim among the fish in the deep oceans. The monster's eyes are, of course, the eyes of three scientists who eagerly photograph and study the intriguing nature of this water-buried world.

Deep Quest is one of several submersibles built within the past few years to journey to the depths of the sea. It is made of strong metal to withstand the tremendous pressures and has moveable parts for collecting specimens, otherwise difficult for man to obtain.

Deep Quest, a 50-ton submersible, looks like a gigantic underwater beast as its mechanical arms reach out for a sample.

The story of submersibles goes back forty years to the American biologist, William Beebe. In 1934 Beebe and an engineer named Otis Barton descended some 3,000 feet into the Atlantic Ocean off Bermuda. They performed this amazing feat in the *Bathysphere,* a submersible of their own design. This pioneer journey marked the beginning of man's travel to all depths within the oceans.

Spurred by this success, two Belgians, the father and son team of Auguste and Jacque Piccard, set out to conquer the very deepest part of the Pacific sea floor. Aboard the *Trieste* on January 23, 1960, Jacque Piccard and Donald Welsh, a U.S. Navy lieutenant, touched bottom in the Marianas Trench, over 35,000 feet below sea level.

A few months later the *Trieste* was challenged again. Its task — to locate the U.S. nuclear submarine *Thresher,* lost in some 8,000 feet of water in the Atlantic. On August 29, 1960, after repeated dives, men aboard the submersible spotted pieces of metal scattered over a wide area. From letters printed on the fragments, the men knew their mission was accomplished. What was left of the *Thresher* had been found.

The *Trieste* had proved its worth. The age of submersibles had arrived. Since then, these man-made fish have performed a variety of tasks. They are used to study fish populations to aid commercial fishing, to explore and recover mineral deposits, to collect deep-ocean samples, to take underwater photographs of marine life and bottom conditions, to perform salvage operations on sunken ships and lost treasures, to inspect submerged drilling equipment and pipelines, and to survey the nature of the sea floor.

Varieties of submersibles are now in use. Most are designed for research scientists who wish to learn more about the fascinating ocean world. *Flip* is a curiosity among these vessels. Neither ship nor submarine, it is a bit of both. A *Floating Instrument Platform, Flip* is towed horizontally to the desired location and then "flipped" into a vertical

Deep Quest prepares to descend as a diver leaves the ship after a pre-dive inspection.

Courtesy U.S. Naval Oceanographic Office

Flip, shown in three positions from horizontal to vertical.

position. Flipping is done by opening tank valves at the tail (stern) end of the vessel. Water fills the tanks, and the weight causes the stern to sink slowly. Scientists then have a stable surface deck as well as a marine laboratory extending 150 feet into the water.

Nekton Gamma, a two-man submersible, serves a variety of uses from inspecting offshore California petroleum production pipelines to coral reef studies along Jamaica.

Courtesy General Oceanographers, Inc.

Courtesy Oceanographer of the Navy

This habitat with four chambers was used during the 60-day mission of Project Tektite 1. The lower right compartment is a "wet laboratory" open to the sea at all times. At the upper right is the engine room. Crew quarters for eating and sleeping are on lower left. The research area is at upper left.

Living Like Fish

For sixty days a team of oceanographers lived among the fish in the eastern Caribbean Sea off St. John, U.S. Virgin Islands. Each day the scientists put on their underwater suits and scuba gear and swam among the coral reefs. They studied the behavior of marine life and the movement of sediment on the shallow ocean floor fifty feet below sea level. At night they relaxed in a four-room, air-conditioned living unit anchored to the bottom where they ate and slept in comfort. This was project Tektite I, successfully completed on April 15, 1969.

Project Tektite really began several years earlier. During the mid-1960's, the Sealab experiments tested man's ability to live under the water for short periods of time. Knowledge gained from these studies has since led to several other projects. One is FLARE, the *Florida Aquanaut Research Expedition*. In early 1972, a team of oceanographers used *Edelhab II* as a home to study the Florida Keys.

FLARE and other projects in progress allow oceanographers an opportunity to observe marine life and sea-floor activity for much longer time spans than ever before. Now one final step remains for man to live among the fish, farming the sea floor and harvesting its resources. He must develop a way to breathe freely under water. He needs a pair of gills.

This diagram shows various ways of examining the ocean. The submersible *Aluminaut* is built entirely of aluminum.

Courtesy Oceanographer of the Navy

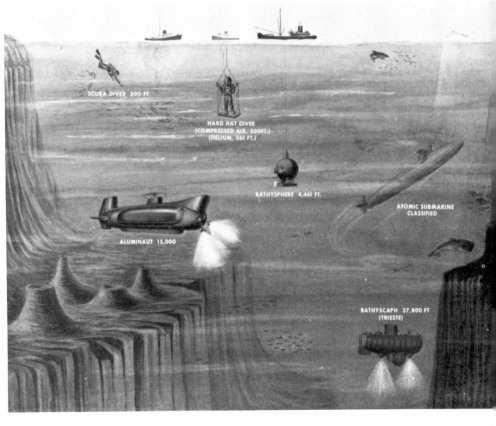

Project FLARE shown with its mother ship above the submersible, *Edalhab* II.

The gills of fish absorb oxygen in the water. In this way fish keep a supply of oxygen in their bodies. Already experimenters have a device which "breathes" water and removes the oxygen from it. Perhaps some-day a machine of this type can be designed so that man-in-the-sea will strap it on and use the oxygen in the water just as the fish do. Some doctors are even considering the possibility of an operation which could add this breathing mechanism to man's body.

Future Use of the Ocean's Surface Waters

In 1965, a bridge was being built across the River Rance near the coastal edge of France, but it was no ordinary bridge, for beneath it a power plant was under construction. One historic day in August, 1966, the gates were closed, the switches turned on, and electricity from a new source surged through the wires to the city of Paris.

Twice each day water rushes inland up the channel of the River Rance, then flows back to the sea as the tidal bulge passes. Under the bridge, this back-and-forth flow of the *tides* turns the blades on a series of turbines. These specially designed machines convert the movement to electricity.

Tidal patterns form as the moon moves around the earth. The gravitational pull of the moon causes bodies of water on earth to bulge. As the earth rotates, these water bulges move onto the shores in the form of tides.

Man has looked to many shallow inlets along coastlines for harnessing tidal power. The Russians have already begun to develop a series of tidal power plants in the bays of the White River in northwestern Russia. The Bay of Fundy, separating the state of Maine from Nova Scotia, also promises to yield such energy for future harnessing.

Bridge and tidal power plant across the River Rance, France.

Courtesy French Embassy Press and Information Division

An "eye," 570 miles high in the sky, looks down on the surface waters of the ocean. From this lofty position, ERTS-1, the first *Earth Resources Technology Satellite*, orbits our planet 14 times each day. Special cameras and scanning devices on board this satellite record views of earth on magnetic tape. A return beam sends the information to receiving stations on earth where pictures can be made.

Contrasts in water temperature, not easily measurable from the surface, are picked up by the satellite. By scanning in the infrared portion of the wavelength of light and recording the images on special film, satellite cameras trace the path of huge North Atlantic cold-water eddies

Courtesy U.S. Naval Oceanographic Office

Oceanographers raise a payload of valuable information from the ocean. On top is a rosette sampler with bottles which were electronically triggered open at different depths to collect water samples. Below is a "bird cage" with instruments measuring depth, salinity, temperature and sound velocity of the water.

advancing south through the Gulf Stream. These eddies may affect patterns of marine life and control location of successful commercial fishing.

Satellites have many uses in oceanography. Perhaps they will serve as the policemen of the seas, looking for the hot water (thermal) pollution by cities and industrial plants that border the coastlines. Oil spills can also be detected immediately by these space observers, and the movement of the oily waters can be followed. Upwellings of cold water with the supply of nutrients they bring to the surface can also be spotted. The space eye can in this way help to locate schools of fish that patrol the near surface in search of food.

A dense cloud cover no longer hides the ocean surface from man's view. Satellites can penetrate these clouds on wavelengths of light that the human eye cannot see. Icebergs no longer hide from unsuspecting ships under a blanket of heavy fog. The satellite picks up these floating blocks of danger and relays their position in time to warn the ships.

11

Your Future in Oceanography

Will our civilization be forced to return to a more primitive way of living because we lack mineral resources to maintain our industries? Will we suffer widespread starvation and water shortage?

Present resources on our continents cannot fill the increasing demands for food, fresh water, and minerals. Perhaps, however, if we utilize the enormous wealth of the oceans, we can enjoy a greater abundance of these necessities than ever before.

Your talents may make the difference! Some of the most challenging careers today's young men and women can enter lie in the many specialized fields that make up the science of oceanography.

Oceanography: A Variety of Careers

Utilization of our oceans calls for the skills of many people in a wide variety of scientific disciplines. Oceanography is a composite of all the basic sciences — especially biology, chemistry, geology, and physics. To solve the many problems in protecting our oceans from pollution and for developing the riches of the seas, numerous other specialists will also be needed. These include engineers, technologists of many types, economists, lawyers, public affairs specialists, doctors, statisticians and craftsmen.

112

Biological oceanographers deal with the astonishing complex of living creatures that inhabit the seas. These biologists may find new food sources through their studies of plankton, seaweed, fish and mammal life.

The problems of "desalting" water and eliminating pollution call for the knowledge of chemists, who may also find a satisfactory way to extract the oceans' minerals. *Chemical oceanographers* treat the entire subject of the nature and distribution of the dissolved substances in the seas, including the materials introduced by man.

Marine geologists seek mineral resources in the oceans that can guarantee our future prosperity. They also regard the seas and the rocks of the ocean basins as a key to unanswered questions about the earth's origin, the development of life, and an understanding of changes which the earth's surface is continually undergoing. Geological oceanographers, along with *marine geophysicists,* study features like buried fracture zones, submarine volcanoes (seamounts and guyots), and the effects of earthquakes on the ocean floors. Their current fascination with the paleomagnetism of the mid-ocean ridges has resulted in a new picture of how the continents evolved.

Through clearer understanding of temperature patterns, density distributions, water circulation, and other physical properties of the oceans, we will be able to use the seas more productively and avoid the dangers of contamination. These are concerns for *physical oceanographers.*

One aspect of physical oceanography is the interaction of the atmosphere and the oceans. *Meteorologists* study these effects and plot the earth's weather patterns. Through their interpretations of observations made by weather satellites and ocean surface measuring techniques, the disasters caused by hurricanes and other storms can be prevented.

The complex problems of sea exploration may be solved by *engineers.* Technology and equipment are needed for deep-sea drilling, submersibles, harvesting the continental shelves, and mining the ocean floor. As our demands for the resources of the seas grow, ocean engineering must expand to apply new discoveries and to design new equipment.

A fresh focus on the whole ocean system is necessary to save all aspects of its life. *Environmental oceanographers* develop methods of preservation for coastlines and continental shelves, and study the life balance of the deep oceans. In the future they will keep records of sea life populations, working closely with other scientists and engineers to

Marine life and man's activities in the sea should co-exist in harmony. Here shrimpers find good fishing near an oil rig in the Gulf of Mexico.

Courtesy Sun Oil Company

Artist's view of a submersible of the future gathering samples from the deep ocean floor.

advise authorities when man's activities harm the delicate balance in the oceans.

Research on marine organisms is a field of growing interest to the *medical professions*. Life in the seas may hold the answer to understanding, and perhaps curing, some of man's most puzzling diseases. Fascinating experiments are being conducted to appreciate the special talents of some sea creatures, such as sharks and whales.

The oceans are an international concern. Cooperative efforts of many countries are necessary to manage the seas properly. *Economists, lawyers, politicians,* and *public affairs specialists* can work for the common interest of mankind.

Training for a Career in Oceanography

Many educational backgrounds can be adapted to a career in oceanography. The high school program should include ample coursework in science and mathematics. It is ideal to have science courses in biology, chemistry, earth science, and physics if possible. These subjects provide a strong foundation for college work.

Oceanographers are commonly highly-trained specialists. College undergraduate training (the four years leading to a Bachelor's degree) is best spent learning the fundamentals of one subject, usually a field of science or engineering. It is generally not wise to get an undergraduate degree in oceanography. Most colleges and universities insist that study in oceanography be a graduate program (after the Bachelor's degree). This requires additional education in order to apply the skills of undergraduate training to the complexity of the oceans.

In graduate school, the nature of courses and the length of training will depend upon the field of oceanography a student chooses. Ample opportunity for "ship time" will be included, for working on oceanographic research vessels in the coastal waters or for going out to sea. A minimum of two years in graduate school is likely, with a Master's degree as the goal. A Ph.D. degree is necessary for some specialties; this usually requires three to five years of graduate work.

More than fifty colleges and universities now have programs especially designed for training oceanographers. Best known are the well-established marine institutes that have extensive fleets of research vessels. These include the Lamont-Doherty Geological Observatory of Columbia University, Woods Hole Oceanographic Institution along the Atlantic coast, and Scripps Institution of Oceanography of the University of California-San Diego on the Pacific coast. In recent years, however, many major universities, especially those along the coastlines, have expanded their courses and degree programs in the fields of oceanography with fine training now available at these schools.

Not all work in oceanography, however, demands this much college training. *Technicians* are vital to the future development of the oceans, and technical skills may be learned in programs lasting from six months to two years. Some high schools offer special courses for technicians and many vocational and trade schools teach a wide selection of these skills. Electricians, photographers, machinists, electronics experts, and construction workers are but a few of the skilled craftsmen who can apply their talents to sea projects.

Many different employers hire people to work in oceanography. Most important is the federal government with major programs under the U.S. Naval Oceanographic Office and the National Oceanic and Atmospheric Administration. State and local governments of states bordering the oceans are developing more extensive programs as interest in coastal waters grows. Universities and non-profit research organizations also employ a variety of oceanographers, although their needs are primarily for highly-trained personnel. Private industries are important employers, and their needs for trained people are expected to rise as the resources of the oceans become increasingly significant.

Our Greatest Gift

The oceans can no longer remain a barely explored and poorly developed mystery. We have a pressing need for materials that only the seas can give. The many secrets still hidden within the ocean depths may well be our salvation. Our exploration and development, however, must be done with caution. The oceans remain the most important resource left on earth. Their protection will preserve the greatest gift we have to pass on to future generations.

Glossary

Abyssal Plain — An extremely flat region beyond the continental rise formed by fine sediments burying the irregularities of the deep-sea floor.

Acanthaster — A red and green, many-armed starfish, known as the "Crown of Thorns" which feeds on corals and has destroyed sections of coral reefs in the Pacific Ocean.

Atlantis — A "lost" continent once thought to exist in the Atlantic Ocean.

Benthos — A wide variety of bottom-dwelling animals extending from the coastal floor to the deep sea which includes barnacles, corals, crabs, sea urchins, sponges, and starfish.

Bromine — An element obtained from seawater for a variety of uses including dyes, gasoline, medicine, and photography.

Continental Rise — The gently-sloping sediments extending from the continental slope base onto the deep-sea floor.

Continental Shelf — The gently-sloping border of the continent between shoreline and steeper continental slope.

Continental Slope — A relatively steep slope (several degrees) beyond the continental shelf extending to the deep ocean.

Copepod — Animal plankton abundant in the sea that consume enormous quantities of plant plankton and are, in turn, important to the diet of many fish.

Coral Reef — A ridge or shelf of limestone (calcium carbonate) formed by the growth of clusters of corals, commonly along continents and islands in warmer waters, especially in the Pacific Ocean.

Desalination — The removal of dissolved material (salts) from seawater to produce fresh water for human use.

Deuterium — A variety of hydrogen, called heavy hydrogen, found in seawater that is important in nuclear reactions like the hydrogen bomb.

Diatom — Single-celled, microscopic plant plankton (algae) that secretes a tiny siliceous external skeleton (shell).

Dinoflagellate — Plant plankton (algae) with whip-like oars for moving; they are important as food for animal plankton.

Distillation — The desalination process of boiling seawater and condensing the steam to remove the dissolved material (salts).

Echogram — Graph of the sea floor shape made by recording water depths by sound wave measurements.

Great Barrier Reef — A coral reef extending over 1,250 miles along the coast of northeastern Australia which abounds with shallow marine organisms.

Gulf Stream — A system of warm surface currents that flows northward out of the eastern Gulf of Mexico along the Atlantic coast to Newfoundland and then eastward as the North Atlantic Current.

Guyot — Steep-sided hills rising off the sea floor with flattened tops.

Humboldt Current — Northward-moving waters along the west coast of South America, kept cold and enriched in nutrients by upwellings from the deep ocean.

Hurricane — A violent tropical storm forming a large spiral or whirlwind with wind speeds of 74 miles per hour or more.

Hydrocarbon — A compound of hydrogen and carbon derived from altered organic matter which forms crude (unrefined) oil.

Longshore Current — Ocean current flowing along the coast formed as waves approach the shore at an angle.

Magnetic Reversal — A change in the north and south magnetic poles of earth (magnetic polar flip).

Magnetometer — An instrument that measures the strength of earth's magnetic field.

Manganese Nodule — An irregular, commonly rounded, mass containing manganese-oxide minerals that forms naturally on the ocean floor.

Mid-Ocean Ridge — A broad mountain range extending along the middle of an ocean basin.

Nansen Bottle — A special bottle used for sampling water at ocean depths. It is open at both ends when lowered to the desired depth, but the ends close when the bottle is flipped over, trapping the water sample.

Nekton — Free-swimming animals such as dolphins, seals, whales, and a wide variety of fish.

Nutrient — Any mineral (compound or ion) used by plants to produce organic matter.

Oceanography — The study of the oceans, including an application of the basic sciences and engineering to the oceans.

Ocean Trench — A narrow, steep-sided trough on the deep-sea floor.

Oil — Liquid hydrocarbon (hydrogen and carbon compounds) formed by decay of organic matter in buried sediments.

Paleomagnetism — The study of magnetism retained in rocks to determine the nature of earth's magnetic field in the past.

Pangaea — A supercontinent of all the present continents which may have existed some 250 million years ago.

Plankton — Weak swimming and floating plants and animals carried by ocean currents. They range from microscopic size to jelly fish.

Salinity — The total amount of dissolved material (salts) in seawater.

Sargasso Sea — A region of clear, warm water in the North Atlantic Ocean that contains floating seaweed, called sargassum.

Seamount — A steep hill or peak rising off the sea floor.

Seawater — The water of the oceans containing abundant materials (salts) in solution.

Species — Related, interbreeding organisms with similar forms which normally do not interbreed with other organisms.

Submarine Canyon — A steep-walled valley cut into the continental shelf and slope.

Submersible — A small ship built to operate underwater and designed for special functions.

Sulfur — A mineral and natural element formed on salt domes by bacteria removing sulfur from other substances. Sulfur is mined by the Frasch method of hot water solution.

Tethys Sea — A large seaway existing between Eurasia and Africa approximately 100 to 250 million years ago.

Tide — Rhythmic rise and fall of ocean waters caused by gravitational pull of the moon or sun on earth.

Tsunamis — Sea waves caused by disturbances in the oceans (earthquakes or sediment slides) that pile up to great heights as they break on shore.

Some Books to Read

Abbott, R. Tucker. *Seashells of North America*. Western Publishing Company, Inc., Golden Press, New York, 1968.

Amos, William H. *The Life of the Seashore. (Our Living World of Nature Series)* Published in cooperation with The World Book Encyclopedia, McGraw-Hill Book Company, New York, 1966.

Bascom, Willard. *Waves and Beaches: The Dynamics of the Ocean Surface. (Science Study Series)* Anchor Books, Doubleday & Company, Inc., Garden City, New York, 1964.

Berrill, N. J. *The Life of the Ocean. (Our Living World of Nature Series)* Published in cooperation with The World Book Encyclopedia, McGraw-Hill Book Company, New York, 1966.

Carlisle, Norman. *Riches of the Sea: The Science of Oceanography*. Sterling Publishing Co., Inc., New York, 1967. (Bantam Book, 1972).

Carson, Rachel L. *The Sea Around Us*. Oxford University Press, New York, Revised Edition, 1961. (Signet Book, 1961).

Coker, R. E. *This Great and Wide Sea — An Introduction to Oceanography and Marine Biology*. (The University of North Carolina Press, 1947.) Harper Torchbook, Harper & Row, Publishers, New York, 1962.

Cousteau, Capt. J. Y., with James Dugan. *The Living Sea*. Harper & Row, Publishers, New York, 1963. (Pocket Book, 1964).

Cowen, Robert C. *Frontiers of the Sea: The Story of Oceanographic Exploration*. Doubleday & Co., Inc., New York, 1960. (Bantam Book, 1963).

Engel, Leonard, and the Editors of Life. *The Sea*. Time Incorporated, New York, 1961.

Gaber, Norman H. *Your Future in Oceanography*. Richard Rosen Press, Inc., New York, 1967.

Golden, Frederic. *The Moving Continents*. Charles Scribner's Sons, New York, 1972.

Gordon, Bernard L., Editor. *Man and the Sea — Classic Accounts of Marine Explorations*. American Museum of Natural History, Doubleday Natural History Press, Garden City, New York, 1972.

Gross, M. Grant. *Oceanography: A View of the Earth*. Prentice-Hall, Inc., Englewood Cliffs, New Jersey, 1972.

Guberlet, Muriel L. *Explorers of the Sea: Famous Oceanographic Expeditions*. The Ronald Press Company, New York, 1964.

Idyll, C. P., Editor. *Exploring the Ocean World*. Thomas Y. Crowell Company, Inc., New York, Revised Edition, 1972.

Marx, Wesley. *The Frail Ocean*. Coward McCann, Inc., New York, 1967.

Matthews, William III. *Science Probes the Earth: New Frontiers of Geology*. Sterling Publishing Co., Inc., New York, 1969.

Scientific American Book. *The Ocean*. W. H. Freeman and Company, San Francisco, California, 1969.

Scientific American Readings. *Continents Adrift.* W. H. Freeman and Company, San Francisco, California, 1971.

Scientific American Readings. *Oceanography.* W. H. Freeman and Company, San Francisco, California, 1971.

Shepard, Francis P. *The Earth Beneath the Sea.* Atheneum, New York, Revised Edition, 1971.

Taber, Robert W., and Harold W. Dubach. *1001 Questions Answered about the Oceans and Oceanography.* Dodd, Mead & Company, New York, 1972.

Yasso, Warren E. *Oceanography — A Study of Inner Space.* Holt, Rinehart and Winston, Inc., New York, 1965.

Index

About the Author

Robert E. Boyer is a professor of geological sciences and education at the University of Texas in Austin, and the recipient of several National Science Foundation grants for teacher training programs. He is also a Fellow with the Geological Society of America and an Honorary Life Fellow with the Texas Academy of Science. He has edited numerous science journals, and has written a great many articles that have appeared in scientific and educational publications. He is also the author of several books and pamphlets.

A native Pennsylvanian, Professor Boyer holds degrees from Colgate University (BA), Indiana University (MA), and the University of Michigan (PhD). He and his wife and their three children make their home in Austin, Texas. In his spare time, Professor Boyer collects antiques and restores Model T cars.